Anonymous

Thoughts on recent scientific conclusions : and their relation to religion

Anonymous

Thoughts on recent scientific conclusions : and their relation to religion

ISBN/EAN: 9783337263980

Printed in Europe, USA, Canada, Australia, Japan

Cover: Foto ©Lupo / pixelio.de

More available books at **www.hansebooks.com**

THOUGHTS ON RECENT
SCIENTIFIC CONCLUSIONS

AND THEIR RELATION TO RELIGION

STRAHAN & CO.
56, LUDGATE HILL, LONDON
1872

[*All Rights reserved.*].

INTRODUCTION.

THE revelations of the hitherto unknown mysteries of the great depths of the ocean, disclosed by the recent deep-sea soundings, and communicated by Dr. Carpenter, have shown that some of the calculations of geologists as to the time represented by certain conditions of fossils and their strata are altogether erroneous; and scientific men now learn that life, which it was confidently asserted could not exist in the darkness of the great deep, or under its great pressure, is actually abundant, and that species identical with species existing in our shallow seas find an existence there. That we should have fallen into such errors, and induction, deduction, and ratiocination (to use the Mill terminology), be found in fault, is not surprising, for astronomers, whose observations and calculations are more within the range of "verification," are waiting for the transit of Venus, to ascertain whether or not an error of four millions of miles (a small fraction indeed of the whole distance) has been made in the calculation of the earth's distance from the sun. The discovery of the remains of pre-historic man under certain circumstances in Western Europe is adduced as proof of his great antiquity, and the revival of the Lamarckian theory, the descent of man from the ape, throws back our origin to a very remote period. Some geologists of the first order affirm, some equally eminent deny, that the operations and forces of Nature have been the same, and of the same magnitude and intensity, from the earliest dawn of creation to our own epoch, and any numbers of thousands of years, heavy "drafts on the bank of time," as Sir C. Lyell calls them, are assumed to be the time required for the accumulations of certain deposits, deltas of rivers, gravel-beds, and the erosion of valleys and gorges. To the consideration of such theories and conjectures the following pages are devoted, in an earnest desire for the elucidation of truth, the object of true science. It must, however, be observed that, inasmuch as some of the theories referred to, and to be considered, are founded upon deductions derived for the most part from conjectures with a minimum of fact to support them, and, from the nature of the case, incapable of verification, the argument must necessarily, in various instances, be confined to showing that the probabilities are as great on one side of the question as the other. The discoveries of Dr. Carpenter show the necessity of not blindly concurring in scientific or so-called scientific conclusions, however eminent the authority which has promulgated them. The views of geologists of the greatest eminence—the loss of one of whom, the late Sir R. Murchison, all geologists must deplore—are so antagonistic on some material points, that the uncertainty of the *vera causa* of certain geological phenomena, unfortunately incapable of actual proof, is rendered still more uncertain. It will therefore, it is hoped, be considered a legitimate occupation, where " doctors differ," to inquire into the subject-matter of their difference, as well as to consider arguments as liable to error as those which the deep-sea soundings have detected.

CONTENTS.

	PAGE
ANTIQUITY OF MAN	1
DRAFTS ON THE BANK OF TIME	28
LA TINIERE	47
PRE-HISTORIC MAN	72
DARWINISM	101
PROFESSOR HUXLEY ON DARWINISM	148
THE DELUGE	243
THE MOSAIC COSMOGONY	285

ANTIQUITY OF MAN.

THE conjectures of some modern philosophers respecting the immense antiquity of the human race have been of late founded upon discoveries made in various places of the juxtaposition of human remains, bones, or implements, with the bones of extinct fossil animals, in gravel-beds or in caverns, above or beneath their stalagmite floors.

Sir C. Lyell tells us*—"That man is, geologically speaking, of very modern origin we may assume, although we have obtained satisfactory proofs that he was contemporary with the mammoth and many other extinct mammalia, and that he has survived con-

* "Principles of Geology," vol. ii. p. 451.

siderable changes in the physical geography of the globe." At p. 74 is a similar statement, but subject to a very important condition—"if their (*i.e.* the fossil remains) geological position has been correctly ascertained."

Sir Charles also informs us of the immense quantities of carcasses and remains of mammoths (*Elephas primigenius* and *Rhinocerus stichorinus*) preserved in frozen sand or mud found in Siberia; also that Tilesius declares his belief that the bones left in Northern Russia exceed all the elephants now living on the globe. We are also informed by Dr. Wiseman ("Essays," p. 223) that the dogs, and even some of the men of the Tungusian chief, Schumakoff, fed upon the flesh of these fossil creatures in 1799. We have therefore before us the fact that the remains of extinct mammalia—extinct, for we know not how many thousand years—may not only be found in juxtaposition with human remains of the present day, but are actually so completely ice-preserved as to furnish food for bears, wolves, &c., and for men who relish them.

It is evident that to a period of intense cold—a glacial period—must be attributed the destruction of those vast herds of mammoths, and that it must have been sudden in its effects is most probable, otherwise the flesh of these animals would have had time to decay and perish, instead of being preserved by frost, snow, or ice; besides, had the intensity of the coldness of the climate been gradual, the mammoths, if endowed with the sagacity of the elephant of our time, would have migrated to a more genial climate.

As the rivers of Siberia rise in the south and fall into the Arctic Sea, it would appear that some great flood had swept away all living creatures from a more genial, though still a cold climate, to the northward into an arctic one. How suddenly they may have been frozen up, Huc, in his "Voyage dans le Thibet," vol. ii. p. 219, has shown, having seen a troop of fifty wild oxen encrusted in the ice, their heads above the surface, their eyes pecked out by eagles and ravens.* But whether the elephants were in like manner suddenly frozen up, or whether they waited patiently for centuries to be by degrees so destroyed, we have the positive fact that their remains are associated with those of recent animals, either in the arctic seas or on the earth, and so completely preserved as to supply food for men and animals many thousand years after their destruction. We

* Sir Charles Lyell's "Principles," vol. i. p. 190.

may also conclude that some day or other a knife may be found under the bones of a mammoth, but we certainly could not extract from its position any proof of the immense antiquity of the man who made it, as is done in the similar case of the flint instruments found associated with mammoth bones.

The geological evidences of one or more glacial periods are numerous and convincing. We have also reason to believe that in the times of pre-historic man a far colder climate prevailed over Europe than at present; as for instance, among other reasons, the bones of the reindeer are found in the South of France. This state of climate would be perhaps the last lingering years of a glacial period, perhaps the same as that which destroyed the mammoths of Siberia. But this or any other glacial period would have destroyed other extinct mammalia—the hippopotamus as well as the mammoth and rhinoceros—and would equally have enclosed them in (it might almost be said) an everlasting preserving case of ice, like the mammoth and rhinoceros of Siberia, and would have supplied food to the then living animals and prehistoric man, as it did to the Tungusians. Therefore the juxtaposition of the remains of men with those of extinct mammalia is no proof of the contemporaneous existence of those men and mammals, any more than the remains of the mammoth, &c., now in the British Museum or that of St. Petersburg, are proofs of our contemporaneity with the ancient mammoth or rhinoceros. Man may or may not have been "contemporary with the mammoth and other extinct mammalia;" but the discovery of his remains associated with theirs, on which the argument for their contemporaneity is founded, is no proof whatever of the fact, or the deduction from it, the great antiquity of prehistoric man, inasmuch as those extinct mammalia may have lived at a time as far removed from the time when the men existed with whom their remains are associated, as we are from the time when the mammoth and rhinoceros roamed in the forests of Siberia. At the same time, as it is impossible to say when these animals perished from off the face of the earth, their antiquity may, after all, not be so very remote, and their extinction may only have preceded by a short time the reindeer of France or Germany, the *Ursus spelæus* perhaps, and other extinct animals now only found as fossils, and which may be considered historical animals, as Cæsar and others have noticed their existence in historic times. The curious and clever sketch of a mammoth upon a bit of mammoth tusk, found in the cave of the Madeleine, in the Dordogne, a copy of which is given in Sir J. Lubbock's "Origin of Civilization," &c., p. 25, would certainly appear to show the probable existence of the mammoth and the artist who sketched it, but it does not amount to a proof of such coexistence. Whole carcasses of these fossil mammoths having been found in Siberia, this sketch may have been taken from one such exposed carcass, as Adams might have made a drawing of the entire carcass he discovered in 1803.*

From the discovery of the fossil remains of extinct animals and of man's supposed contemporaneous existence, Sir John Lubbock says, "The fauna of the country [in northern

Lyell's "Principles," vol. i. p. 184.

France] must have been indeed unlike what it is now. Along the banks of the river ranged a savage race of hunters and fishermen, and in the forests wandered the mammoth, the two-horned rhinoceros, a species of tiger, the musk ox, the reindeer, and the urus." Does the presence of the bones of the mammoth and rhinoceros,* mixed as they must be with some human reliquiæ at the present day in Siberia, justify this positive assertion? As well may it be said hundreds of years hence, when present facts shall have been forgotten—"The fauna of Siberia *must* have been indeed unlike what it is now. Along the banks of the rivers (Lena, &c.) ranged a race of Russian hunters and fishermen, and in the forests wandered the mammoth, the rhinoceros, &c."

* " Pre-historic Times," p. 308.

The flint implements found in the valley of the Somme, near the Reculvers, and many other places in different parts of the world, at considerable depths under gravel-beds, are alleged as a presumption of the great antiquity of our race. In the first place, it is necessary to consider in what manner such gravel-beds are formed. These beds consist of fragments of flint, quartz, &c., some rounded and rubbed smooth, but principally broken and angular, and mixed with silt and sand. The effect of flowing water upon stones, whether that of a river or of the tide, is to round the edges and smooth the surfaces, and form what is usually called shingle—a process not requiring any great length of time, as we know, by finding on sea-beaches, and in rivers' beds, rounded fragments of very recent glass bottles and hard stoneware. But gravel-beds, unlike shingle, are composed of a large proportion of broken angular stones, much like what is found in the plain of débris at the foot of a glacier. Sometimes, interspersed, are found large transported blocks, which may have been borne along on a moving calotte of snow or glacier, or floated to their present position upon, or encased in, blocks of ice, or carried there by violent floods, such as that of the valley of Martigni. The great gravel-beds, therefore, are probably due to the combined or separate action of ice and floods. "Glaciers cover many thousand square miles in Iceland, descending from the mountains and pushing far into the lowlands. This tendency of the ice to encroach has very materially diminished the habitable quantity of ground."* These glaciers necessarily push before them great

* Mrs. Somerville's "Physical Geography," p. 192.

quantities of ground and broken rock or gravel.

It is supposed that, from the identity of the flora and fauna of England and those of the Continent, there must have been a communication between them. Mr. Damon, in the "Handbook of Geology of Weymouth," p. 152, says—"Professor E. Forbes has shown that the animals and plants of living British species are chiefly of Germanic types, and could only have found their way hither by strict communication with the Continent overland. The greatest sea depth between Weymouth and Cape la Hogue is 45 fathoms, between Dover and Calais 30 fathoms. Supposing the bed of the channel raised 100 ft., a bar which crosses from the coast near Newhaven to Dieppe would be dry land."

There is also a tradition that the island

Lomea existed somewhere in the upper part of the English Channel, and also that the Goodwin Sands were once an island, the property of the Earl of Goodwin; nor is there any difficulty in accounting for their destruction, as we have the instance of the Scroby Sand, once an island and the subject of litigation, utterly destroyed in a single gale, and also eight out of fifteen islands of Zealand swallowed up by the sea, *temp*. William Rufus. When the borings were made in the Goodwin Sands, with a view to the erection of a lighthouse upon it, the solid chalk was found at a depth of 80 ft., a chalk ridge, the nucleus of the sands. It is not improbable that this ridge, like the Needles or the projecting chalk pillars near Swanage, may have been connected with the chalk cliffs of Ramsgate. The degradation of this 80 ft. of chalk might be the work of a few years in a period of intense cold as compared with degradation under a temperate climate, which would be the work of as many centuries. Dr. Kane has shown in his "Arctic Explorations" (see p. 29) how rapidly such degradation is effected in the present "glacial period" of the Arctic regions. Possibly this degradation may have been assisted by some such convulsive action as that which forced up the great chalk cliffs at the Needles at nearly a right-angle to their original position, and also possibly broke the continuity of the chalk deposit between the island and the opposite coast near Swanage. This may in some measure give a countenance to the tradition. Tradition, encumbered as it may be with extravagances, has probably a certain foundation of truth, and although not altogether trustworthy, is certainly as valuable as conjecture. If then we suppose the channel between Dover and Calais (its greatest depth being only 30 fathoms), closed by a connecting isthmus either wholly or in part, by an island, or blocked up with the ice of a glacial period, the English Channel,—or La Manche, its more descriptive name,—would then have been much in the condition and shape of the Bay of Fundy. There the tide rushes in with great violence and rapidity, and is raised in some parts of the bay to the height of nearly 100 ft.

At present the great Atlantic tidal wave, checked by the western coast of Normandy, rises there to the height of 45 ft.; and in the Bristol Channel, where it flows into the estuary of the river Severn, to about 60 ft. How much greater, therefore, would be the rise and fall of the tide in the funnel-shaped

English Channel, if it were closed, like the Bay of Fundy, at its extremity between Dover and Calais, by an isthmus, by ice, or if it were much reduced in width by an island. The rise of the North Sea flood-tide would also, but perhaps in a minor degree, be greatly increased. During the glacial period, therefore, the tides rising to a much higher level than at present, would have drifted icebergs or floes not only up and down the Channel, but also up and down the rivers and estuaries falling into it, such as the river Somme; at one time heaping up, at another throwing down, masses of gravel, into which they had converted the shingle or rolled stones of the rivers, and bearing with them the bones, with or without the frozen flesh, of ancient fossil animals, as the Siberian fossil mammoths must now be floated, ice-borne, up and down the rivers of Siberia. Now supposing a mitigated glacial period, or rather a very cold climate, the termination of that period in which man and the reindeer existed on the banks of the river Somme, and suppose these men to have made their flint instruments on its banks. We must infer that considerable floods invaded the river from the melting of the snow, &c.; and we know that rivers, protected even by art, will, under such circumstances, destroy their sides or embankments, washing everything on the surface away into the bottom of the stream. The flints, knives, &c., would then be found at the bottom of the river, and, subsequently, floods or travelling ice-floes would operate to bury them at any depth beneath where they were originally deposited.

An illustration of this method of accounting for the discovery of the buried remains of human art is afforded by Mr. J. Ferguson, who says in a paper on the recent changes in the delta of the Ganges:—" From these data it will be perceived how fallacious any conclusions must be which are drawn from borings in the strata of deltas, and indentations formed from local superficial deposits. I myself have seen the bricks which formed the foundation of a house I had built carried away and strewed along the bottom of a river at a depth of 30 or 40 ft. below the level of the country. Since then the river has passed on, and a new village now stands on the spot where my bungalow stood, but 40 ft. above its ruins; and any one who chooses to dig on the spot may find my reliquiæ there, and form what theory he likes as to the antiquity of my age."*

This treatment of the mystery may likewise account for the absence of human *bones*, together with the flint implements, as we may easily conceive the submersion of these implements without inferring that of the manufacturers—a fate they would as easily have avoided as the tenants of Mr. Ferguson's house. Thus there does not seem any reasonable proof of the antiquity of man to be derived from the discovery of flint implements at the bottom of, or at any depth in, drift or gravel-beds associated or not at such depths with fossils of extinct animals. Nor does the depth at which these implements are found give us any reliable measure of their antiquity,

* "Biblical Antiquity of Man," Rev. S. Lucas, F.G.S., p. 240.

as that which was originally on the surface may have been washed far away and buried deep below its original position.

Many a fine merchant-ship has been swallowed up in the quicksands of the Hooghly. In scarcely more than forty-eight hours a vessel of 800 tons has entirely disappeared, leaving a hollow instead of a sand-bank as would be supposed. To what depth such a ship sinks into the earth it is impossible to say, but the very least that could be suggested would be some 40 or 50 ft. The depth, therefore, of the sepulture of such a ship and any of its contents, would be no measure of their antiquity, if at some future period the Hooghly should shift its bed, and some philosopher should dig and find them. Or, if some hundred years hence, no record or tradition of the great earthquake of Lisbon of

1755 were preserved, and that on sinking a well or mine near the spot where many hundred persons crowding for safety were swallowed up, there should be found their remains, yet their depth below the surface would afford no measure of their antiquity. In Asia, Italy, South America, and many other parts of the world, such calamities are recorded. How many more must there have been which are not recorded! We may therefore find remains of animals of man or of his works in strata of any period, possibly, and not improbably, without any concomitant evidence of the earthquake which placed them there. I have been informed that a philosopher, very liberal with millions of years, found the relics of a wine or beer-bottle imbedded in gravel many feet in depth. To the great rise of tide may be attributed many of the raised beaches on our coasts, without having recourse to suppositions of upheavals of the earth's crust, local or general. And this rise of tide, combined with the wearing and grinding of icebergs and floes, may explain more rationally the wearing away of hard rocky cliffs, such as is seen near Dartmouth and elsewhere, than by assigning it, as I have heard *ex cathedrâ* in a lecture, to the action of the waves, the eroding action of which is considerably checked, if not prevented, by the growth of sea-weed, or by mussels, limpets, and other shell-fish. In the same way the rocks in the bed of a river are commonly protected from abrasion by some kind or other of a slimy lichen.

Nor does the discovery of human remains of any kind with fossils in caverns under thick beds of stalagmite afford any proof of the

ANTIQUITY OF MAN.

antiquity of our race. For it is evident that if bears,—who delight in caverns,—wolves, and other animals, are now feeding upon ancient ice-preserved mammoths, and no doubt they drag portions of them into caverns, if caverns there be, on the river Lena and other Siberian rivers, we may fairly presume, looking back to ancient times, that the carnivora of those days did the same with the ice-preserved animals of the same or some previous glacial period. Parts of them may have been washed or dragged in in a frozen state, not only with the integuments, but even with the flesh entire, and thus the presence of the two joints of the bear's leg of the Brixham cave is accounted for without any necessity for inferring the co-existence of the bear with the makers of the flint knives found in the same cavern, or in immediate contact with its remains.

If we further consider the greater rise of tide before suggested, and the denuding effects of calottes or plains of moving snow and glaciers streaming down through the valleys of Brixham, and Kent's cavern, besides the action of floods, we have every reason to assume that the bottoms of those valleys once stood at a much higher level than at present, so as to admit of currents of water passing through these caverns, not to mention streams from melted snow through the now silted-up swallow-holes on the surface, which cuttings expose to view, otherwise concealed from our view by the stalactitic formation on the roof of the caverns. The absence of human bones from so many of these caverns is accounted, or rather apologized, for by the analogous absence of any such remains at the bottom of the now desiccated Haarlem lake, although battles were fought on its waters. Bodies of men and animals after a certain number of days become inflated with the gases of putrefaction and rise to the surface. The bodies of the victims of the battles on the shallow lake would have been drifted, after rising to the surface, to its shores, and if not then decayed or buried, as they probably would be, the bones would be found there, and not in the bottom of the lake. Sunken ships, cannon-balls, &c., are not found, probably because they have sunk too deep into the bottom of the lake; and as some of these relics of the battles, which must be there, may hereafter be discovered, they will afford additional proof that the depth of the burial of any work of man is no measure of his antiquity. A shovel and hammer which were lost in the first inspection of the bottom of the Thames by the diving-bell for the construction of the tunnel, were afterwards found buried 18 ft. below the surface of the river's bed.*

The absence of human bones in the cultivated bottom of the Haarlem lake, affords no suggestive explanation of their absence from the caverns. But a thick floor of stalagmite covers some of these remains of fossil animals associated with flint and other implements. Surely it is as easy to suppose that the men who made these implements may have used these ancient ice-preserved animals for food, as did the Tungusian chef and his followers; or, inasmuch as the thickness of the stalagmite is the growth of time, that thickness a few thousand years ago must have been very much less than now, and an accidental blow, or the fall of a heavy block of stone from the

* Lucas's "Biblical Antiquity of Man," p. 234.

roof of the cavern, may have made a hole through which the implements might fall or be washed under the bed of stalagmite. Even where a second stalagmite floor may have been formed from the accidental closing or desertion of the cavern, the same circumstances may cause us to marvel at the associated remains of the works of man and of fossil animals, but by no means allows us to adduce this association as a proof of man's co-existence with extinct fossil animals, and of his great antiquity.

DRAFTS ON THE BANK OF TIME.

THE immense periods of time—millions of years—constantly assumed as necessary to account for denudations, accretions of deposit, &c., appear in many cases unnecessarily heavy "drafts on the bank of time." Sir Roderick Murchison* has shown the fallacy of the arguments which attribute the denudation of the valley of the Wealden to denuding operations lasting, according to Darwin, some 300,000,000 years. It is assumed in these calculations that the degradation proceeded at the same rate as at the present day, *i.e.* under exactly the same

* Murchison's "Siluria," p. 493.

circumstances of climate, temperature, &c., during enormous periods of time. But it is universally acknowledged by all geologists that we have satisfactory evidence of the existence of a glacial period, if not of several, and its effect in the rapid denudation of cliffs, probably of a harder substance than chalk, is abundantly proved by Dr. Kane in his "Arctic Explorations" (vol. ii. p. 223). "As we travelled with our empty sledges along a sort of broken track or road which led under the cliffs, I realised very forcibly the influence of the coming summer upon the rocks above us. They were just released from the frost which had bound them so long and so closely, and were rolling down the slopes of the débris with the din of a battle-field, absolutely clogging the ice-belt at the foot. Here and there too a large sheet of earth and rocks would leave its bed at once, and gathering mass as it travelled, move downward like a cataract of ruins. The dogs were terrified by the clamour, and could hardly be driven on till it intermitted. But it is not in the season of thaws only that these wonderful geological changes take place. Large rocks are projected in the fall, by the water freezing in the crevices, like the Mons Meg cannon-balls." We have no right to assume that the valley of the Wealden, twenty miles wide, was one continuous mass of chalk from cliff to cliff. Nor can we be sure that earthquakes or landslips may not have contributed to facilitate the work of denudation in the course of a few centuries. Who, contemplating the present city of Lisbon, would venture to assert, without knowledge of the fact, that such a fearful earthquake as that of 1755 had well-nigh destroyed it? And what do we know of the periodical alternation of earthquakes in ancient times, when we know so little of it in even modern historical times, though we see their effects in the vast rending of mountains in various parts of the world?

Mr. J. W. Tayler,* describing the fiords of Greenland, says, "The lofty mountains, rugged, precipitous, and barren, with patches of ice (projections from the great interior glaciers), and snow unmelted by the summer's sun; with valleys half filled up by enormous angular blocks of stones detached from the sides of the steep mountains by the alternate frosts and thaws; the solitude, and the almost total absence of life, animal and vege-

* Proceedings of the Royal Geographical Society, Jan. 28 and Feb. 21, 1861.

table, make up a picture of indescribable desolation."

The valleys which open into some of the fiords of Norway, now rich with vegetation, show unmistakably that at some former time they presented the same appearance as the valleys of Greenland. They were in the same manner half filled up with an immense heap of fragments of rock and detritus, the remains of which are visible, more or less, in many a valley. That of the valley at the end of the Eid Fiord, one of the branches of the Hardanger Fiord, is grandly conspicuous, now intersected by a river, and divided into terraces, probably due to the action of water, and the glacier which once ground over it, leaving moraines and a tent-like mound on its upper surface, and the neighbouring rocks striated and furrowed by the ice. The terraces formed in these valleys are attributed by some geologists to the action of the sea, rather than to the action of ice and torrent. The terraces, however, on the banks of the river Wye, near the spot where Sir R. Murchison first laid his finger on the Silurian formation, cannot certainly be attributed to the action of the sea, and they have a strong family likeness to the terraces in Norway and elsewhere. We have, therefore, ample reason for the supposition that the valley of the Wealden had its share of this violent action.

Sir C. Lyell estimated the time required for the accumulation of the mud, &c., forming the delta deposits of the Mississippi at about 67,000 years, and founded these estimates upon calculations and experiments relating to the quantity of sediment contained in the water in 1866, and an assumed average depth of the fluviatile formation. So that this estimate is founded on the assumption that the average annual amount of deposit was the same during a vast period of time. But there must have been a time when the level of the river was below instead of above the surrounding country, the banks of the river, now about 15 ft. above it, having been the gradual work of the river itself by the deposits left and arrested by vegetation at every rise or overflow in times of floods. Of necessity, therefore, the washings of the surrounding country must have poured into the river a far greater amount of mud, sand, and silt, than now, and a still greater amount when the earth was bare of vegetation and forests, for it is to be presumed forests and vegetation had a beginning. When we add to this the effects of a glacial period and the enormous floods which every thaw must have produced, as we see in nearly every valley in Norway, and even in many others of England and of Scotland, surely the calculations made from the amount of deposit at the present time cannot give a fair average estimate of the time required for the formation of the delta. Sir C. Lyell gives a sketch of the ravine near Milledgeville, Georgia ("Principles," p. 344), excavated in twenty years 55 ft. deep and 180 ft. broad, and says, "When travelling in Georgia and Alabama, in 1846, I saw in both these States the commencement of hundreds of valleys in places where the native forest had recently been removed." We have direct evidence, therefore, of the effects of the absence of forests. The contents of these valleys must have been washed away somewhere, either into rivers or lakes, and add to their deltas to an extent far greater than when the native forest existed. The probability, therefore, of similar effects should be taken into consideration in all these calculations; there may be other effects, such as quantities of blown sand from a parched surface. It does not seem true philosophy to found any argument upon so uncertain a basis. The same may be said of the delta of the Ganges, and of the calculations as to the number of centuries required for its formation. Mr. Ferguson's estimate is a period of 5,000 years, while Colonel Strachey suggests 13,000. To the other difficulties in making anything like a trustworthy, even approximate, estimate of these accumulations of river deposits, an additional unknown quantity, resulting from possible elevations and depressions, such as that of the "sunk country" of the Mississippi, must be taken into consideration.

What dependence can be placed on the calculations made of the time required for the recession of the cataract of Niagara? Mr. Bakewell, from information given him by the first settler who had lived there forty years, supposes that recession to have proceeded at the rate of 3 ft. per annum. Sir C. Lyell came to the conclusion that "the average of 1 ft. a year would be a much more probable conjecture." He tells us "that that part of the chasm which has been the work of the last hundred and fifty years resembles, in depth, width, and character, the rest of the gorge which extends seven miles below." The depth and character would naturally be the same at whatever rate the recession proceeded; but the largest cataract —that is, the *width* at the falls—is "more than a third of a mile, or 586 yards 2 ft. broad," not to mention the smaller one of 600 ft.; whereas the rest of the ravine "varies from 200 or 400 yards in width from cliff to cliff." One would therefore conclude that from this difference between the width at the falls, no less than from nearly 400 and 200 yards, the work of the last hundred and fifty years can scarcely be said to resemble in width the work which cut through the ravine. I think that part of it where the whirlpool rages, and where once apparently the river seems to have fallen over, is also wider than the rest of the ravine. It cannot be called a far-fetched supposition to attribute the origin of the ravine to a fissure caused by a subterranean movement, such as that of 1811-12 in the sunk country near New Madrid, some few thousand or hundred years ago—a fissure on a larger scale than those described by Sir Charles in his "Second Visit to North America," vol. ii. p. 235 :—"I traced two of them (fissures) continuously for more than half a mile. . . . . I might easily have mistaken them for artificial trenches if my companion had not known them within his recollection as deep as wells." The river, with the help of the severe winters of the climate, especially in a glacial period, which Professor Charles Martins (*Revue des Deux Mondes*, 1867) supposes may have prevailed in the time of man on earth, would have made short work of cutting out the ravine (see p. 42), and the process would be slower in proportion as the water increased the width of the ravine.

But it is said that the horizontality of the strata at both sides of the ravine is so perfect that there are no signs of an upheaval which would destroy the horizontality. If indeed the horizontality is so perfect and the strata not "inclined at so slight an angle that they would be termed, in ordinary geological language, horizontal,"* it does not follow that the horizontality destroyed by an upheaval may not have been restored gradually by a slow subsidence while the river was performing its task of widening its path. Such upheavals and subsidences are very commonly conjectured to account for many a geological phenomenon. The immense period of sixty-seven thousand years as the duration of the work of the river, from the cataract to Lake Ontario and its corollary, the great antiquity

* "Principles of Geology," vol. i. p. 118.

of the present crust of the earth, may be a great mistake. Sir C. Lyell, anticipating the above suggestion as to an original rent or fissure subsequently enlarged by the action of the river, such rents, be it remembered, being common in every rocky country, says:— "There is no ground for supposing that the excavation was assisted by an original rent in the rocks, because there is no fissure at present in the limestone at the falls, where the moving waters alone have the power to cut their way backwards."* This seems anything but a valid objection. The moving waters would "cut their way backwards" not only at the end of the fissure, but at the sides adjacent to it, and thus the head of the rent may long since have been obliterated by the water and winter's ice and frost; for their

* Lyell's "Travels in North America," p. 31.

effect, together with the constant humidity from the spray, in the destruction of the rock, would tend to enlarge the head of the fissure to a greater degree than the rest of the ravine. Or the rent may have had two heads, divided by the higher ground of which the island formed a part of it, as much of that may also have been cut away, and thus we may account for the fall on the American as on the Canadian side. The very bird's-eye view of the river given in the "Principles," vol. i. p. 338, shows two lateral or transverse rents or fissures on either side of the ravine; an "original rent in the rocks" is therefore not improbable, to say the least. But, rent or no rent, if the Simeto in the course of two centuries has eroded a passage from fifty to several hundred feet wide, and in some parts 40 or 50 ft. deep, the rock moreover cut through consisting of a homogeneous mass of hard blue rock, as Sir Charles tells us (*ibid.* p. 357), the Niagara River, without such rent, may have cut its way through the softer rock of its channel in a comparatively short time, assisted by a glacial period, and a climate of far greater severity than that of Sicily. Sir R. Murchison ("Siluria," p. 496) "dissents from those who would account for the production of all valleys and gorges by the action of the water that has flowed in them." This instance of Niagara may be fairly considered one of the cases of rivers in which, as he says, they "simply flow in the gorges prepared for them by previous geological disturbance" (p. 498, *ibid.*).

Any one seeing the vast terraces heaped up hundreds of feet high in the valleys of the Norwegian fiords, with, in some instances, the remains on the highest level of ancient moraines and tent-like mounds, the exact counterparts of those at the foot of recent glaciers, or, to come nearer home, ancient terraces composed of drift and boulders, evidently brought down by the violent action of ice or water, or both, far above the level of the present river-banks, which may be observed more or less in many a mountain and many a lowland valley in Great Britain, will scarcely be persuaded to believe that the forces which heaped up these vast masses were not greater and more violent than those which are now in operation in the same regions, and that, consequently, though there may have been a gradual diminution in the force and rapidity of denuding agencies of all kinds as age succeeded age, any calculations founded upon the basis of the annual rate of deposit at the present day cannot fail to be deceptive.* To compare great things with small, the Rhineland of the present day, with its terraces above terraces, the handiwork of man, substituting for the sterile rock bright and luxuriant vineyards, seems to resemble the great work of the Creator, who, before vegetation was in existence, prepared the earth for its production and the living creatures it was to sustain, and changed the arid rock, by denudation and disintegration, into the vast garden of earth—a process which, once com-

---

* "On several mountains I visited, stones exposed to the atmosphere were crumbling. On Mount Cunningham I had satisfactory proof of it. Small mounds of stone, that have evidently crumbled off the larger mountains, may be seen lying at the base. The winters are doing their levelling work and doing it rapidly."—CAPTAIN HALL'S *Life with the Esquimaux*, p. 35.

pleted, would appear to require, like the Rhinelander's vineyard, only occasional and trifling restoration as compared with the first efforts.

LA TINIÈRE.

ANOTHER "heavy draft upon the bank of time" is drawn by Sir J. Lubbock, from the observations of Mr. Morlot on the cone of gravel and alluvium built up by the torrent of the Tinière near Villeneuve. A railway cutting exposed three layers of vegetable soil, each of which must at one time have formed the surface of the cone. The first ancient surface, 4 to 6 in. thick, containing tiles and a Roman coin, occurred at a depth of about 4 ft. below the present surface. The second layer, 6 in. thick, at a depth of 10 ft., contained fragments of unglazed pottery and a pair of tweezers in bronze. The third layer, 6 to 7 in. thick, 19 ft. below the present surface, contained rude pottery in fragments, charcoal, broken bones, and a human skeleton with a small, round, very thick skull. Taking the Roman period of the first layer at sixteen to eighteen centuries, from the measure of that layer from the surface, he deduces the time required for the deposition of the whole cone at about eleven thousand years.* Further on, at p. 324, he estimates, on the same data, an antiquity of " more than a hundred thousand years" for another cone above, about twelve times as large, formed when the Lake of Geneva stood at a higher level.

The calculation appears to be an erroneous one, or greatly exaggerated. The average annual rate of deposit during the Roman

* Sir J. Lubbock's " Pre-historic Times," p. 317, &c.

period is by no means to be taken as a fair estimate of the previous average annual rate. For even supposing during these thousands of years the same amount of rainfall, cold, &c., in proportion as the torrent enlarged its bed, by the wearing away of the sides of the ravine at every flood on the melting of the winter's snow, so in proportion the violence of the flood and its power of carrying down gravel and alluvium would be diminished, as the flood-waters of a torrent in a confined space necessarily rush down with greater impetuosity than in an open space. In some confirmation of this view, it may be observed that the deposit between the Roman layer of soil and the one below it appears to be 4 ft. thick, the layer below this again about 6 ft., and the lowest layer 9 ft. thick, showing that a larger quantity of gravel and alluvium was deposited in the earlier periods. But the layers of vegetable mould seem to indicate periods of repose, and the large transported blocks found in the alluvium are evidence of the violent action of a raging torrent, when probably these layers were considerably denuded; and although it may have taken sixteen to eighteen hundred years to throw up the cone since the time when the Romans cultivated the surface, it is surely more probable that when the ravine was narrower, as it must have been in the earlier periods, the amount of alluvium brought down in the earlier periods would have been greater, and deposited in less time. For the same reason the cone above, twelve times as large, would also have required proportionately less time for its deposition. If to this we add the effects of a glacial period, we may calculate upon a deposition of far greater rapidity. In fact all these calculations of immense periods of time, founded upon causes now in operation or upon the present conditions of the surface, are of very questionable value, especially when we consider the violent action which results from a period or periods of intense cold, which we have reason to think may have reached the times of pre-historic man in the West of Europe.

In addition to the experience we have of the very rapid rate at which deposits of alluvium may be formed at every return of the summer's heat in the arctic regions, we have also evidence of another extraordinarily expeditious mode of forming these deposits where vegetation is absent, observed by Mr. Collins.*

* "Travels of a Pioneer of Commerce," p. 395.

"Here we stopped. . . . The guides called my attention to the clouds, which were now approaching the pass. Just above it towered an enormously high peak; and when the cloud reached the peak it immediately seemed to dissolve into smoke, and a peculiar subdued roar reached our ears. In a very few minutes a white line showed the water tearing down the mountain to join the stream, a hundred yards from which we were camped; and presently, with ever-increasing roar, the body of water forced its way past us. As the torrent rushed down the valley, it tore up the bed of the original stream, excavating a deep channel for itself, some 30 ft. deep and 50 ft. wide, with banks formed of earth and stones as if piled up by navvies. In less than an hour all was still again and the stream running quietly at the bottom of its enlarged bed. . . . . . In an hour, however, I reached the pass, and to my amazement found that the peak had been reduced into a huge mound, shorn of two-thirds of its height, while both the eastern and western slopes of the mountain were torn up and strewn with the débris in the shape of boulders and stones."

Here we have direct evidence of violent action and extraordinary excavating power, under special circumstances. We find "banks formed of earth and stones" thrown up in former days by our rivers; but this violent action has long ceased, and the beds of all rivers seem now to retain almost the same depth from year to year, the diluvium of the flood-waters being levelled and gradually carried to the sea during the absence of floods.

The reckless destruction of the forests in the time of anarchy in France has been the cause of the destruction of much valuable land, by the washing down of the surface of the bared hillsides on the plains below.

These partial instances show that before vegetation grew on the mountains and hills, a far greater amount of alluvium must have been washed down from hills and mountain-sides, and their valleys and gorges, than in these days. Vegetation now covers nearly every mountain-side, and the degradation of mountains is as a general rule arrested.

We are surely justified in assuming that some of these masses of alluvium of the Tinière, and of so many other valleys and rivers, are—like the groovings and scratchings of the rocks, the results of which form part of these masses—due either to the absence of vegetation or to a glacial period; and therefore, if we confine ourselves to the supposition that the upper cone was the product of that period, and perhaps many years after it, until the naked mountains had produced or reproduced their conservative vegetation, which the glacial period had destroyed, can any reliable estimate be formed of the time required for its deposition by any calculations derived from the eighteen hundred or two thousand years' accumulation since the Roman period? The hundred thousand years of Sir J. Lubbock seems a most unreasonable conjecture.

Even assuming that the formation of any part of the lower cone were independent of any action due to the glacial period, we are not justified in estimating the time of formation of the earlier and lower from that of the upper part.

It was commonly said at Naples that the surface of a lava stream, which of course utterly destroys everything beneath it, would become fit for cultivation in about sixty years. The layers of vegetable mould in the cone must have required probably a lesser period of time. The existence of the three distinct layers of vegetable mould would seem to show that there were three periods of rest, at which the torrent for some cause or other ceased to pour down its alluvium, or discontinued the heaping up of the cone during those periods. It is therefore not improbable that these layers of mould were covered, not gradually, but by the violent action of the torrent, leaving the rate of progress of the construction of the cone still more difficult to ascertain. As a rule, one would conjecture that the rate of the deposition of detritus and alluvium in every river, great or small—the Nile, Mississippi, or the Tinière,—must decrease in proportion as the width of their beds are increased. To this must be added an exceptional increase by a lowered temperature, which we may be certain was the case at some remote period, and the more rapid denudation of the soil in the absence of vegetation.

It does not follow as a matter of course that the skull found in the lowest layer of vegetable mould belongs to the period of its accumulation.

M. Boucher de Perthes, vol. i. p. 190-3, says, "De ces trois morceaux (haches en pierre) du plus beau poli et d'une parfaite conservation, deux sont en silex gris blenté et l'autre en jade vert. Ils étaient ensemble dans ce sable bleu, à 7 mètres environ de la superficie et à $2\frac{1}{2}$ mètres audessous du niveau de la Somme. . . . . A 6 mètres environ de l'endroit où étaient les haches, mais moins profondément, un ouvrier déterra une petite statuette en ivoire, de la hauteur de 8 centimètres, d'un assez bon travail, représentant un homme tenant une palme et une sorte de gril; c'étaient probablement un Saint-Laurent. Cette figurine, qui paraissait provenir des remblais, appartenait au Moyen Age. Je ne le cite ici que comme renseignement." If we were unable to assign a period to this statuette, we might be led into the error of supposing it to belong to a far earlier period. Mr. Ferguson's house, before referred to (p. 18), furnishes an additional commentary on the antiquity of buried remains.

Much has been made of the discovery of the Engis skull in a cave as a proof of a different race of men of a degraded type, and of course of great antiquity, but, according to Louis Figuier, M. Gratiolet produced the skull of a modern idiot closely resembling the Engis skull. An extraordinarily-shaped skull was found with Roman remains in the ruins of Uriconium. Had it been found in a cave by itself, the discovery of another race of man might as well have been proclaimed, as in the case of the Engis skull.

Mr. P. O. Cunningham, in the "Natural History of the Straits of Magellan," p. 179, remarks on seeing two Fuegians, one "hideously ugly," the other with "decidedly good features." "Travellers, I suspect, often draw erroneous conclusions as to the type of face which prevails in a tribe or nation, from having only seen a few representations of it, and the same, no doubt, holds good with regard to the examination of isolated examples of crania."

To enter fully into the geological convulsionist and uniformitarian dispute would be beyond the scope of this work. Sir R. Murchison's twentieth chapter of "Siluria" will satisfy most readers of the reasonableness of his views, and he has an advantage over most geologists, in that some of his theoretic views and predictions have been borne out by facts. It seems, however, that our entire ignorance of the workings of nature under circumstances of which we have no experience, makes our conjectures or deductions of very doubtful value. When a vast portion of the earth's surface was under water, as in the Silurian epoch—when tremendous masses and veins of molten granite or plutonic rock penetrated the strata of the primary and secondary, scarcely at all in the early tertiary, and none whatever in the more recent periods—when vast masses of metamorphic rock were elaborated and of limestone crystallised—when we find "that there is a great difference in the mineral character, generally, between the igneous rocks of the older periods of the world and those at present formed, few will doubt."* We have evidence of a different condition of things in the earlier elaborations of the crust of the earth, which would assuredly lead to the conclusion that we are not justified in assuming that the course of Nature's operations has been the same in the recent as in the earlier periods of the earth's physical history.

* De la Bêche's "Geological Manual," p. 136.

It may indeed be a considerable matter of doubt whether it is necessary to assume such very enormous periods of time for the formation even of mountain masses of stratified rock. In the Silurian series, which Sir R. Murchison has shown to cover vast tracts in almost every part of the earth, we find trilobites and other fossil mollusks in strata separated by immense masses of other but lifeless strata of the same kind. If the deposit of mud, now converted into slaty rock, had been gradual, and proceeding at the rate of a fraction of an inch per annum, one would suppose that fossils would be found succeeding one another continuously; but this not being the case, it may be conjectured that great masses of the mud were thrown down from time to time in quantities sufficient to destroy all life, followed by periods of comparative repose when life would appear, again to be followed by other destroying floods of mud, either by the action of rivers if dry land was then in existence, or if not, by subaqueous mud volcanoes or other submarine action, for we are utterly ignorant of Nature's working in the great abysses of the ocean.

The same may be said of the Red Sandstone, old and new, throughout enormous thicknesses of which no traces of life are found at all. For instance, "The sandstones (of the Vindhyan series of strata in the central provinces of India) are false-bedded and beautifully rippled on their surfaces, each successive bed, often for hundreds of feet in thickness, showing its own ripple-marked surface. Nor is there anything in their mineralised condition to suggest the chance of subsequent obliteration of organic remains, had they ever become embedded or become fossilised. Yet no success has hitherto rewarded our most careful searching for such traces of early existence."*

These long lifeless periods would, one must suppose, interfere largely with "progressive development by natural selection."

Sir William Denison † says that, sailing along the coast of India from Mangalore to Cannanore, they were nearly poisoned by the smell of the sea. "At Cannanore I was told that this was always the case after the southwest monsoon. The quantity of fresh water poured into the sea from a long line of coast, upon which from 120 to 180 inches of rain fall in three months, is the mode of accounting for

---

* "Gazetteer of the Central Provinces of India," by C. Grant. Introduction, p. xxix.

† "Varieties of Vice-regal Life," vol ii. p. 135.

this; the sea becomes nearly fresh water, the salt-water fish are killed, as also the sea-weed, and the water, under the action of a tropical sun, becomes very offensive till it is mixed with the general body of sea-water and resumes its saltness. We saw thousands of dead fish floating on the sea, and the shore was covered with them." It may be concluded that much mud is brought down also with the rain, and that the shellfish share the fate of the fish. Here, therefore, we have one mode of accounting for the great beds of shells, &c., found buried in ancient strata. Sir William Denison repeated this disagreeable experience the following year. "We found the sea as offensive off Beypore and along the west coast as it was last year off Cannanore."[*]

[*] Vol. ii. p. 202.

Year after year, therefore, the south-western monsoon must be forming beds of shells, &c. Storms or currents on the coast may indeed wash away much of the deposit of the monsoon, but some relics would surely be left at the bottom of the sea, and others washed up upon the beach. In the Silurian strata, and in the Red Sandstone especially, there are great intervals without any traces of life. Was this the result of a continuous flow of rain, a continuous monsoon, which prevented the return of life? If such a conjecture be correct, there is good reason for supposing a much more rapid accumulation than any of those going on at the present day.

I wish I had reason to believe in the calculations which have been made in reference to the annual rate of deposits of mud, sand, or silt, which have formed the great Silurian and other deposits. I have a covered reservoir of about 7 ft. diameter, with an average flow of apparently clear water into it, of about three-quarters of an inch, constantly filled by a stream flowing over a Silurian formation. This stream has, in the course of one year of a dry season, left a pure deposit of nearly 4 in. of impalpable mud in the bottom of the reservoir, and much more in a wet season, guarded though it be, as far as possible, from the admission of anything but what is held in suspension by the water. I cannot, unfortunately, therefore look forward to the accumulation of $\frac{1}{15}$rd or some such suggested minute fraction of an inch of mud during subsequent years, and if my reservoir could be transformed into an ocean into which one or more proportionally large rivers or submarine mud volcanoes poured their floods continually, I might fairly expect an annual amount of deposit far exceeding that in my reservoir.

The warping of land is an artificial mode of accumulating alluvial strata, and may be considered analogous to the similar operations of Nature in the deposition of the grea masses which now form mountains of slaty rock such as the Silurian. Each flood-tide flows over the land and deposits the mud held in suspension by the water, but it is necessary to allow the water to return to the river, on the ebb, to prevent the silting up of the drains. A portion, therefore, of the mud in suspension, must be carried away. The average amount of deposit appears to be about 2 ft. in three years. Sir Charles Lyell says, "By repeating this operation, which is called 'warping,' for two or three years, considerable tracts have been raised, in the estuary of the Humber, to the height of about 6 ft."* Warping would not certainly be worth the outlay if the accumulation were only $\frac{1}{8}$rd of an inch annually, nor have we any reason to suppose that Nature's warping was so slow, or that her deposits were not only equal to, but perhaps far greater, than those which are the result of our warpings, the layers only reduced in thickness by the superincumbent pressure; and yet we find layers, apparently little consolidated, containing the most perfect casts of shells, and shells also, unaffected altogether by pressure, beneath masses of lifeless strata in a more consolidated state.

The Persian Gulf affords one instance of the rapid growth of deltas and the accumu-

* "Principles," &c., vol. i. p. 570.

lation of strata, which certainly shows that the calculations derived from present annual increase and the result, immense periods of time required for their formation, may be wholly erroneous. "It is certain that the alluvium at the head of the Persian Gulf now grows with extraordinary rapidity, and not improbable that the growth may have been more rapid than it is at present. Accurate observations have shown that the present rate of increase amounted to a mile each seventy years, while it is the opinion of those best qualified to judge, that the average progress during the historic period has been as much as a mile in every thirty years."*

Sir R. Murchison says, "That the former physical agencies were of the same nature

---

* "The Five Great Monarchies of the World," by G. Rawlinson, vol. i. p. 5.

as those which now prevail, we simply assert, on the evidence of fracture, dislocation, metamorphism, and inversion of the strata, and also on that of vast and clean-swept denudations, that these agencies were from time to time infinitely more energetic than in existing nature," &c.*

From the foregoing observations, it is submitted that the conjectures of immense periods of time, to account for the accumulations of strata and other deposits, may be immense exaggerations, and are of very doubtful value in the interpretation of the geological record.

* " Siluria," p. 490.

PRE-HISTORIC MAN.

THE date of the beginning of authentic, or quasi-authentic, history, varying greatly in different regions of the earth, the term "pre-historic" must bear a very different signification in different parts of the world—a very great antiquity in some of them, a comparatively recent period in others. Setting aside the sacred character of the Old Testament, we have in it a history the truth of which has been proved wherever proof could be found; but accurate chronological deductions cannot be made from it, partly on account of the varieties as to figures in the different versions (and no wonder, considering the extreme antiquity of the book and the liability to error in transcription of the Hebrew notation of figures), partly on account of the genealogies being evidently in some cases those of particular races and not of individuals, besides our ignorance of the manner in which they were traced. A remarkable instance of this is seen in the Gospels of St. Matthew and St. Luke, which are so different, and must have been perfectly intelligible to the readers of them in the first ages of Christianity, or surely would have been explained to prevent any question of their truth.

"Kennicott has fully shown how frequent in the Masoretic text are the mistakes in numerals by letters, some of which from their close resemblance are easily mistaken one for the other," and in a note at foot of the page, "Kennicott adverts to another method of expressing numerals, viz., by short perpendicular strokes for the units, another mark for *five*, and then similar perpendicular strokes for the hundreds. He thinks that the mistakes in the numerals may have arisen, many from this method of notation, some from the words written at length, and some as above mentioned from the letters used as numerals." See also the note at same page referring to Mr. Layard's discovery of some bowls among the ruins of Babylon, with inscriptions written in the old Hebrew character, in which certain numeral letters cannot be distinguished from one another.*

The words or affix which we translate "son of," means often the grandson or descendant. Even in the Greek Testament the Jews say

* Lord A. Harvey, "On the Genealogies of our Lord," p. 222.

"Abraham is our father," and "he also is the son of Abraham." The "Genealogies" also speak of nations or races as descendants, from which it is clear that no certain chronology is deducible from the chronologies. It may be as well to remark, in the words of Dr. Pusey in a letter to the *Times* of Nov. 16, 1870,—"That even assuming the higher antiquity of man, the truth of Holy Scripture is in no way concerned with these theories; that those who hold that antiquity should not allege it as contradicting Holy Scripture, nor allege Holy Scripture as contradicting it, since Holy Scripture, fairly interpreted, said nothing definitely on the subject."

The Egyptian, Indian, and Chinese histories may possibly go back with some degree of accuracy to an early period of the world, about 2000 years B.C., but beyond that they are clearly mythical dreams. All these histories apply to Eastern nations, but what is the commencement of the historic era in the West of Europe? We have, in fact, nothing of any authentic value dating from before a few hundred years B.C. Even the early period of Roman History, 753 B.C., is involved in doubt; and Greek History, if a little earlier (1st Olympiad, 776 B.C.), has the additional disadvantage of being the produce of the more fertile than truthful brains of the mendacious Greek. The historic age of all Western and Northern Europe beyond Italy is still more recent, and it is with pre-historic man of these parts of Europe which we have to deal. The historic age of America is scarcely four hundred years old. It appears, however (taking a general view), that civilisation in the earlier days of the world's history has proceeded from the warmer zones of the earth, and this holds good even in America —Mexico, Yucatan, and Peru having been there the centres of American civilisation, that is, if civilisation is to be measured by the splendour of architectural monuments. That this civilisation in Western Europe came from the Eastward, will hardly be questioned, and that it spread gradually from Asia, Westward, the traditions of the Greeks, of the migration of Atys and others, render very probable. Micali, in his "Italia avanti li Romani," has endeavoured, but without much success, to trace back the origin of Italian races before the Romans. The names alone of some of them remain, the Sicani, supposed to have been driven into Sicily; the Umbrians, and other tribes; and the Etruscans, whose language is still absolutely dead, unless Sir

W. Betham's Celtic derivation is to be credited; but in many of the monuments, pottery, tomb-paintings, &c., the Greeks have left their mark, in the pottery especially, on which are found Greek inscriptions and Greek Homeric subjects. A disgusting worship, almost identical with that practised in India to this day, seen in a tomb-painting of Tuscany, indicates an Eastern derivation. The wave of population seems certainly to have proceeded from the warmer regions of Asia to Western Europe. The migrations, then, from the Eastward of more civilised races than the earlier settlers they came to supplant, better armed, and better organised, would drive out or reduce the latter to slavery. The tribes so driven out in a destitute condition, or the escaped slaves, would, like the wretched slaves of the Southern

United States, who took refuge in miserable swamps out of reach of their masters, have fled across the Alps into Switzerland or France, and been compelled for their subsistence to make use of the simplest tools which came to their hand, such as flint and bone instruments, just as the most civilised race of modern Europe would be compelled to do if cast away in a state of destitution. These tribes, or, in their beginnings, a few individuals, fathers of tribes, may be the pre-historic men of Western Europe. These, again, may have had their victories over others; and by the process of expulsion, as it may be called, by internecine quarrels, for which the climate of Gaul seems so favourable, or by emigration, have gradually spread into the northern regions of Europe, Great Britain, &c., as the wretched Esquimaux appear, according to

Egede, to have been driven to the arctic regions from more genial climates. Cæsar seems to have found the British a nation in a very barbarous condition, notwithstanding the advantages they must have derived from the Phœnicians, and perhaps Greeks, who visited their shores. No doubt a tribe, having learnt the use of bronze for their weapons, would probably soon master and destroy the tribe confined to instruments of stone or wood.

This method of accounting for pre-historic men of the West and North, though a conjecture, has at least the advantage of bearing some degree of analogy with what we know of historic man; for we find the Celtic races, the British, for example, driven Westward into the mountains of Wales by the Romans, from whence some of them probably passed over and peopled Ireland, and probably Scotland. The Bretons and the Basques are found in the extreme West, driven there probably by the Gaul in a similar manner. In the Mediterranean, again, we find Eastern Greeks or Phœnicians settling on all the shores of the Mediterranean. The small-handed races, whom we now find in the East, seem also to have furnished their quota to the West, as we discover so many instances of the short-hilted swords. Again, we do not find proofs of the existence of any large populations among pre-historic men, with the doubtful exception perhaps of the Swiss lake-dwellers and of the people of the Danish Koggen-middens. As far as the former is concerned, the conjecture of their migration from Italy is faintly confirmed by their numbers, Italy having been at an early period very thickly peopled, to judge from the innumerable ruins of towns found in almost every part of the country. Like the modern Swiss, the refugees would have found a comparative security in their mountains, and from thence thin out into farther Western and Northern regions. A slight confirmation of the conjecture that they derived their origin from the Eastward may be alleged from the discovery of jade and other Oriental productions in the lake-dwellings; however, it is equally possible that these Eastern products may have been objects of barter. On the whole, it seems almost certain that pre-historic man of the West and North derived his origin from historic man of the East, and must certainly therefore be considered of a lesser antiquity, as the necessity of migration from the East would only have been felt when the populations of the East had grown to dimensions exceeding the means of subsistence—the principal, if not the only cause of such migrations. Such, we must suppose, was the incentive to the later incursions Westward of the Northmen in England and France—the peopling of Iceland. A ripple of the great Westward flow of the wave of population is to be found in the attempt of the Danes to colonise America (Vinland) in the tenth century, and their subsequent disastrous colonisation of Greenland.

If, therefore, historic man of the East, with the exception of the Jewish race, can only pretend to an antiquity of, at the outside, 2000 years B.C., the introduction of pre-historic man to the West must certainly be of a very much more recent date. Nor can we find, as has been shown, any argument for his great antiquity in the juxtaposition of his remains with extinct fossil animals, or their burial under gravel-beds, or in caverns with or without such juxtaposition.

If any one will consider what his position, even as a man of general education, or even a scientific man, would be if driven naked out of house and home into a wilderness, he will be persuaded of the difficulties to which he would be put to provide himself with the simplest cutting instrument. Even if he should find himself in a country of ironstone, how would he set about the process of smelting and then working the iron without hammer? To make bronze he would acknowledge to be perhaps altogether beyond his powers, even if he were lucky enough to fall in with, and had technical knowledge to distinguish, tin and copper ore. If in a chalk country, without iron, tin, or copper, he would find some difficulty in the manufacture of flint implements. Bronze Roman axes are found of much the same pattern as those of pre-historic man. Are we to suppose that the Romans or other more civilised races than the pre-historic man of Gaul copied the barbarian invention? It seems more probable that the pre-historic exile or refugee adopted, in the construction of his axe of stone for want of other material, the form which he recollected, or which, may be, he brought with him, and handed down the same to his successors.

The theory of a stone, bronze, and iron age, each one preceding the other by a vast lapse of time, appears to be a conjecture of little value. For is it not pretty certain that, as within the last few hundred years, and perhaps even now, stone, bone, and wooden implements were the only weapons and tools of many a savage nation, so there were probably many degraded savage nations such as now exist, probably the outcasts from quasi-civilised nations, who used no other implements, and yet might be contemporaneous even with the Romans of the Augustan age, or at an earlier period, with the civilised nations of the East? Mr. Llewellyn Jewitt, in his "Grave-mounds and their Contents" (p. 16), says, "Another example from Rondisay Hill of a bronze dagger, a barbed arrow-head of flint, and a beautiful drinking-cup." Again, "In a barrow at Paccelly Hay was found a fine axe-head of stone and a bronze dagger, (ibid., p. 26); again, "The Gristhorpe coffin contained among other things three flint flakes, a fragment of a ring of horn, a small implement of wood, and a bronze dagger," (ibid., p. 48); and, finally, "The articles which the grave-mounds and cemeteries of the Romano-British period most frequently produce are (among other things) arms both of bronze and of iron." To this may be added that flint arrow-heads have been found about Roman camps. From these examples we may surely infer that bronze and stone, and bronze and iron, were used indiscriminately by the people to whom the grave-mounds belonged, the less civilised making use of stone at the same time that the more civilised used bronze or iron, or both. Thus the Germans of the Rhine make use largely of brass pots and pans, while ours are of tin or copper. The discovery of lake-dwellings, standing alone, affords no evidence of any great antiquity. They were *institutions* in Scotland certainly in the time of the Romans, in Iceland within the last 400 years, and in Africa to this day, according to Captain Burton. Nor can the quantities of very rude flint implements afford any satisfactory evidence of the existence of a very ancient savage race. The mason's hammer is a rude implement compared to the carpenter's or the jeweller's. May not the rude flint implements have been used for coarse and heavy work, the less rude ones the implements of a poorer class, the finer ones those of the wealthy, and have been all of the same period. The accumulations of refuse by Fuegians and Australians are the Kjökkenmöddings of our day, and the relics of ancient Danes, Scotch, or British, found in buried forests, afford no substantial proofs of any enormous antiquity; for, according to the great authority of Sir R. Murchison, the vertical stumps of these forests, instead of affording indications of long and slow action, are evidences of a sudden movement,* and he cites the eminent Dr. Forchhammer, who very rationally "argued that the rapid immersion of the trunks, and their having been quickly surrounded by marine mud, could alone have preserved them; for if the trees had been gradually sinking at the rate of an inch or two in a year, they would have been entirely decomposed under the atmosphere long before their submergence, and thus no trace of their trunks would have remained."

The savage races do not certainly present the progressive development of beauty or intellect, and it would seem more probable

* "Siluria," p. 491.

that they are degenerating into, rather than that they should have proceeded from, the Simian genus, if there be any truth in development theories. The supposition of an island within the tropics as the original seat of man is, as certainly contrary to all history and tradition, more valuable than mere guess and conjecture. The Duke of Argyll has in his "Primæval Man" sadly undermined, if not completely disposed of, the "Savage Theory" of Sir J. Lubbock, which supposes the primæval man a savage. This theory, like many others of the present day, seems to be useless, a mere guess, not admitting of any kind of verification, drawing very largely upon conjecture, very little upon history or facts. Taking a general view of the globe, it appears that the extremities of the great continents have been the refuges of the outcasts of the earth—the Cape of Good Hope, with its Hottentots; Terra del Fuego; Australia; in the southern; the arctic regions; all, or nearly all, of the high latitudes in the northern hemisphere; also outlying islands in both hemispheres; every discovery of new lands in these regions during the last two or three centuries has shown us nothing but tribes of savage people without a semblance of the progress we call civilisation. If the primæval man was a savage, and civilisation gradually proceeded from him, how is it that every one of these tribes of savages was found in the savage state, though isolated and left to their own devices, like the primæval savage? Some one of them ought surely, with plenty of time before them, to have acquired the art of at least one of the three R's. How is it that the Fuegian, exposed as he has been for centuries to a fearful climate of cold and tempest, has not yet made any progress towards the attainment of the simplest arts bearing on his comfort? Why was the wretched Tasmanian so utterly degraded as to have lost or never discovered the art of making a fire, and the Australian savage scarcely superior to a beast as far as civilisation is concerned? The history of man seems to show that degradation, as much as progress, has been his true condition—"the badge of all our race." History shows us that the whole of Europe north of the Alps is indebted, at all events for its first germs of civilisation, to the Italians or Romans; the Romans and their predecessors, the Etruscans, to Greece; the Greeks to Asiatic peoples, and not improbably, or in part at least, to the Jews; for we find Tatian asserting that the Greeks derived their learning from the barbarians, and Clement of Alexandria, in the "Stromata," showing from Aristobulus and Numenius, that Plato and Pythagoras drew their philosophy from Hebrew books, and that Pythagoras was a plagiarist of Moses.

The progress of improvement in the West has been but slow; the civilisation in the Middle Ages, in some respects, inferior for many a century to that of the imperial Romans; even Benvenuto Cellini regarded the Parisians as little better than barbarians, and the English still worse; and Burton's interesting "Life of Simon, Lord Lovat," shows that even the Highlanders at that time were not very far removed from the savage state. The Irish native, in the time of Elizabeth, seems to have been as nearly a savage as possible. The first great strides of progress began apparently with the invention of printing, and the arrival in Europe of many Constantinopolitan Greeks at the time of the Mahomedan conquest. Steam power by land and sea, the electric telegraph, and the resultant facility of communication between nations, are now causing gigantic strides in civilisation in Europe and North America.

But let us look back to the history of the Eastern nations of the Old World. There, instead of progress, we find evidence of degradation. The industrious Chinese have been long in a stationary state, and much inferior to their ancestors, whose grand works they cannot or do not imitate. The magnificent ruins of Nakon Wat stand "like a mighty sphinx frowning contemptuously on the infantine and barbaric state of the arts and science of the people who are now the denizens of the forests and plains in its vicinity."* The Hindus are equally degenerate. The great empires, Nineveh, Babylon, having fulfilled the predictions of the prophets of the Bible, are desolation. The Egyptians, the Copts, and all Asia, are more or less in a very degraded state. The curse of Ham seems ever to have bowed down the miserable African. The savages of Africa are for the most part as primæval as ever, or perhaps in a worse state than that of the primæval savage, making a guess at his condition; and not even the communication with civilised men has had as yet much effect, nor the influence of Mahometanism, which is so

* Mr. D. O. King, in "Journal of Geological Society," vol. xxx. p. 183.

far in advance of fetishism and savagery, in introducing an advance in the arts and morals of civilisation.

History therefore seems to show that civilisation, or the arts, its physical and moral accompaniments, beginning somewhere in the East, has been always passing slowly Westward from one part of the earth to another—a process which is still going on; and now that the time is arrived when, as the prophet Daniel says, "man shall walk to and fro over the earth, and knowledge shall increase," we may hope for a renewed progress over the whole world, if not checked by evil influences, the parasites of civilisation, or by the outrageous anarchical doctrines now prevailing among sections of the peoples of the West.

The account therefore of the Bible, concise as it is, considered as a history with only the same authority as of other histories, appears to be far more consistent with all that we know of human progress (little as is that knowledge) in archaic times, than the conjecture of the "primæval savage," for in the Bible we learn that in the very beginning of man's history there were men endowed, as we must suppose, with superior intellects, who discovered and made known to the world many of the arts which contributed to the civilised condition of human beings.

We have, however, in the history of the Pitcairn Islanders, almost a direct proof of how easily and how soon the descendants of a civilised race might become savages. After all the fathers but one of the settlers on the island, some of them educated but evil men, had perished by murder or otherwise, leaving a tribe of descendants almost in a savage state,

Adams, the surviving father, repented of his evil ways, and with the inspiration of Christianity and the Bible, infused a wonderful degree of order, and a very remarkable amount of real virtue, into the islanders, although they were much behindhand in all the material arts of civilised life, scantily supplied as they were with the tools and appliances of civilisation. Can we for a moment suppose that, had it not been for the spirit of religion which shed its beneficial influence upon Adams, those immediate descendants of civilised man would not have fallen into complete savagery?

The Pitcairn Islanders were indeed for a long time absolutely cut off from communication with the rest of the world, but the segregation of tribes or individuals by the moral barrier of hatred or fear, which would be continually compelling them to fly into the wilderness, or the physical barrier of mountains, such as the Alps, of rivers, or of seas, would, as in the case of the Pitcairn Islanders, as completely deprive them of the advantages of communication with the tribes or nations of a higher civilisation from which they, like the first Pitcairn settlers, had escaped or had been expelled and compelled to migrate out of reach of their enemies. Many an American tribe is now undergoing the same process, notwithstanding the anxiety of the United States' Government to treat them with all humanity. Such humanity was by no means a feature in the characters of the Greeks and Romans. Slavery or death was the doom of the conquered.

The coarser flint instruments may represent

a neolithic age, but may equally have been the instruments used for coarser purposes or by the poorest of the tribe, while the finer ones were the property of the chiefs or the richer individuals. They may be of a remote antiquity, but probably of an antiquity less remote, as far as the West is concerned, than the historic period of the East. The use of iron and bronze may have been fashions of individuals, tribes, or nations. The destruction of iron by oxydation being very rapid, and that of bronze very slow, bronze implements may be found while their contemporaneous iron implements may have long since perished. Generally speaking, it may be said that the distinction of a stone, bronze, and iron age, cannot be accepted with any degree of certainty, and comes within the misty region of conjecture.

DARWINISM.

MR. Darwin's theories of the origin of species by progressive development, by natural selection, &c., involves the consideration of a very remote antiquity indeed for *genus homo*.

"We thus learn that man is descended from a hairy quadruped, furnished with a tail and pointed ears, probably arboreal in its habits, and an inhabitant of the Old World."* A large fossil monkey having been discovered in Miocene strata, his conclusion is, that we are the descendants of some kind of baboon at some period long anterior to the Post

* Darwin's "Descent of Man," vol. ii. p. 389.

Pleiocene period, and "Thus," he says, "we have given to man a pedigree of prodigious length."* Professor Huxley † says that Darwin's "explanation or coincidence of observed with deduced facts, is, as far as it extends, a verification of the Darwinian view." "As far as it extends" is a very loose qualification of verification. Adopting Mill's terminology, inductions and ratiocinations we have in copious abundance, and Mr. Darwin's arguments remain in that stage of investigation, but not one single "verification" of his conclusions is to be found, if verification means not a mere inference from observed facts, but some positive proof of the truth of the inference; for the best of reasons, that a "verification"

---

* "Descent of Man," vol. i. p. 213.
† "Lay Sermons," &c.

of Mr. Darwin's theory is simply impossible, as we can never attain to any proof whatever of the truth of his fundamental principle that mankind and all animals have descended from one, four, or five primordial forms. Many of his facts he often admits are doubtful. His views are not new. They are but a *réchauffé* in a scientific crust of ancient conjectures, no doubt suggested by the same similarities which seem to have influenced the Darwinian views. The faun of antiquity with pointed ears and tail, the satyr, centaur, dryads, sea-nymph, merman and maid, &c., must now be considered representations of realities, not mythological or poetical fictions. Darwin thus states his view in the " Origin of Species," p. 484, "from analogy, that probably all the organic beings which have ever lived on the earth have descended from some one primordial form into which life was first breathed by the Creator." Again, in the same page, "I believe that animals have descended from at most only four or five progenitors, and plants from an equal or lesser number." In the last page he repeats his notion of the descent of organic beings from "either a few forms, or one into which life was originally breathed by the Creator," and at page 489 we read, "as all the forms of life are the lineal descendants of those which lived long before the Silurian epoch, we may feel certain that the ordinary succession by generation has never been broken."

According, therefore, to this view, from some one Eozoon, Ascidian, or primordial form, or four or five, all organic beings, genera and species, have proceeded in some order or other, as from mollusks to fish, fish to birds, birds to reptiles, reptiles to quadrupeds, and, finally, from ourangs or gorillas to man, in "the ordinary succession by generation," progressive development by natural selection, the struggle for existence, sexual selection, evolution, &c., one or all, the *modus operandi*. In support of this view, we are also furnished with arguments derived from the similarity of totally distinct genera in the embryonic stage. Mr. Darwin has collected a number of facts relating to the similarity of structure in that stage, and also relating to rudimentary structures. "The homological construction of the whole frame in the members of the same class is intelligible, if we admit their descent from a common progenitor, together with their subsequent adaptation to diversified conditions. On any other view, the similarity of pattern between the hand of a man or monkey, the foot of a horse, the flipper of a seal, the wing of a bat, &c., is utterly inexplicable. It is no scientific explanation to assert that they have all been formed on the same ideal plan."* He acknowledges, however, that "It is notorious that man is constructed on the same general type or model with other mammals."† And again, "With respect to development, we can clearly understand, on the principle of variations supervening at a late embryonic period, how it is that the embryos of wonderfully different forms should still retain, more or less perfectly, the structure of their common progenitor. No other explanation has ever been given of the marvellous fact that the embryo of a man, dog, seal, bat, reptile, &c., can at first sight hardly be distinguished

* "Descent of Man," vol. i. p. 31.   † Ibid., p. 10.

from each other."* It can hardly be said that we *clearly* understand the retention of these structures, especially after the supposed immense lapse of time from the common progenitor, or why, if indeed they are absolutely identical in the different embryos, they should not have shared in the changes they have all undergone in other subsequent stages of growth for thousands of years.

May there not be another conjecture as plausible as that of the common progenitor to account for the marvellous fact that the embryos of man, dog, seal, &c., can "*at first sight be hardly* distinguished from one another?"

"It is notorious that man is constructed on the same general type or model with other mammals."† That is to say, the

* "Descent of Man," vol. i. p. 32.　　† Ibid., p. 10.

Creator has ordained that certain chemical and mechanical and other laws, together with the inscrutable law of life, shall operate in the construction of all mammals. As therefore the man, dog, seal, &c., are evidently constructed on the same general type or model in the adult stage, the *a fortiori* conclusion, without, or antecedent to, any observation, would naturally be that the embryos also would be on the same general type or model. Again, the variations in the germs or ovules of these different mammals would be imperceptible, and as the growth is gradual, in another stage they would *at first sight* be *hardly* distinguishable, but as their growth continued, so their variations would become more and more apparent, until they culminated in the adult creatures.

Mr. Darwin seems to infer that the variations supervene only "at a late embryonic period." It seems more probable that they should be continually going on from the first germ in gradual steps, though too minute and gradual for our detection in the earlier stages, rather than that they should suddenly supervene at any particular stage. Admitting the fact of a "general type or model" of creation, it seems nothing extraordinary that parts or limbs of different mammals should also partake of the same typical plan, or that there should be a similarity of pattern between the "hand of a man or monkey and foot of a horse," without any other "common progenitor" than the Great Artificer who designed the model. If it be scientific to assert that all mammals have been formed on the same ideal, plan, type, or model, surely it is as scientific to assert that these parts of these mammals are also formed on the same ideal, plan, type, or model. If the whole machine of animal structure is of the same model, it seems probable that the parts of such structures should necessarily be also of the same model.

Notwithstanding this apparent similarity of the different creatures in the embryonic stage, the experience of thousands of years has shown that in the adult stage they invariably lose that similarity, and as invariably assume the respective forms of their parents — a constant invariable law as far as we are able to judge. Mr. Darwin's theory is in direct opposition to this law, as according to that theory the embryo of the one, four, or five progenitors and their descendants must have assumed in the adult stage, not species only, but genera also, in numberless cases different forms from those of their parents. It would therefore appear more probable that, instead of one, four, or five progenitors, there must have been legion.

With respect to rudimentary organs, as for instance the mammæ of men. The male and female being constructed on the same model, it seems as rational as the conjecture of a common progenitor to suppose that up to a certain period the embryos of male and female are of the same model, that at another the functional arrangements are arrested when the embryo is destined to be a male, the organ remaining in a rudimentary state.

But are we quite certain that some rudimentary organs in man analogous to those in animals may not have served some purpose in his embryonic stage, though apparently useless in his complete development? are we quite certain that they are even then useless—may they not be for the purpose of adding beauty to the form, or may there not be other causes which we know not and can never know? Can we, for instance, pretend to assert that the vestige of the spinal chord found in the *os coccyx* is useless in the embryonic stage? As a great general law, we see in the vast field of creation an almost universal adaptation and use of everything created; it is therefore more probable that such organs are not useless, and that it is our ignorance which pronounces them to be so. Even in the case of deformities, we may presume that they subserve some use or other of which we are ignorant. It may be said this is no scientific explanation; but science and common sense must agree that there is an infinity of inexplicable things in Nature, beginning with the first grand difficulty, creation—its end and object; and Mr. Darwin, to do him justice, in many cases admits our ignorance. Sir C. Lyell, referring to Lamarck's "Philosophie Zoologique," says:— "Among other facts, the abortive teeth concealed in the jaws of some of the mammalia are mentioned, such teeth not being required, because their food is swallowed without mastication. The discovery also by G. St. Hilaire of teeth in the fœtus of the whale is alluded to, and the small size of the eyes of the mole, which scarcely makes any use of its organs of vision." Is it true that the mammalia swallow *all* their food without mastication? Some of them certainly masticate bones and vegetables, *faute de mieux*. As full license is given to conjecture, the following may be hazarded. If mankind were killed off before coming to maturity, and before the wise tooth had grown, man, as one of the mammalia, would be said to have abortive teeth concealed in his jaws. May not this be the case with some other mammalia, and these abortive teeth intended for use in an advanced stage of life, which their many enemies rarely if ever allow them to attain? Does every, we might almost say any, man who kills a very old mammal examine the jaw to see if there is any sign of growth in these abortive teeth? As for the mole, it is incorrect to say that he scarcely makes any use of his organs of vision. Moles are not only seen sometimes abroad in the daytime, but must often be above ground at night or at dusk in search of other quarters; his organs of vision therefore are of considerable use. As all living creatures are constructed on the same type or model, and as the organs of vision are an essential part of the model, the *Proteus anguineus*, to which he also refers, has such organs, but undeveloped. It may be necessary for such development that light should be required, which, in the lakes within the caves of Styria and Kentucky, is wholly absent. The caves of Kentucky also contain the cave rat of Professor Silliman, with greatly enlarged eyes, the converse of the Proteus, probably because it is not confined to total darkness in the water of the subterranean lakes like the Proteus, but may occasionally wander into parts of the caves where some degree of light penetrates. We do not make development theories on the eyes of owl or cat, why should we do so in cases which appear to us exceptional? We might as well attribute any or all of our organs to use or disuse.

When we consider, admire, and wonder at the marvellous adaptation of every living creature, from the minutest insect to the largest mammal, to the purpose for which it was created, is it not a rational conclusion that these apparent exceptions, the rudimentary organs, do subserve some object of which we are ignorant? What, it may be said, is the use of the lavish amount of beauty of form and colour in the animal and vegetable world? Mr. Wallace, I think, in one of his works, expresses surprise at the extraordinary amount of beauty of insects and plants, wasted, as it were, unseen and unappreciated in the solitude of tropical forests. May it not be that, as in the arts as well as Nature, beauty is in fact only appreciated by the few of a higher natural or cultivated intelligence? so, there may be far higher intelligences, capable like ourselves, but to a far greater degree, of admiring and enjoying the wonders and beauty so lavishly displayed in the works of the Creator, many of which are not appreciable by our lower intelligence or deficiency of our organs of sight, many hidden from us in the microscopic world as well as in the unknown solitudes of the mountains, forest, desert, or impenetrable depths of the ocean.

We are told that owing to the imperfection of the geological record, the links which unite the different genera are missing, that here and there instances, such as *Simocyonidæ*, *Hyænitis ancylotherium*, in Miocene strata, *Archæopteryx* and *Campsognathus*, in the Oolite, are supplied, but inasmuch as these supposed links are few and far between, while their number, if they existed at all, ought to be very great, and therefore ought to be found at least in the same proportion as other fossils, we have every right to assume that we presume too much on "the imperfection of the geological record." We may therefore continue without fear to classify genera, preserving as they do throughout all time their distinguishing features. But why are we to seek for these supposed links among fossil animals? We have these apparent links between the snake and the lizard, in the different Sirens (*Siren anguinea, Lacerta anguinea, Chalcidis lacerta*), some with two, some with four diminutive legs and various numbers of toes; also the carpet snake of Australia, with "two little horny legs, scarcely discernible, on the belly near the vent;" but we have not the smallest proof of any one of these changing into either extreme of the chain—the snake or the lizard.

It is then assumed that "natural selection," with a sufficiency of millions of years, will produce such a development and effect the change. This is mere assertion without proof; indeed, the proof is the other way, for the last few thousand years are a part of the aforesaid million, and, "natural selection being always at work," one or more instances ought to have been detected even within the last one, two, or three hundred years. "Natural selection," however, would have little chance of success, for it is difficult to believe that any animals should have enjoyed all the advantages demanded for progress in development by natural selection during a million of years continuously, in the face of all the probable changes of climate and circumstances on the earth's surface during such a lengthened period. One genus we may suppose to have enjoyed a very lengthy enjoyment of all the advantages of "natural selection," the genus Cestracion, but seems to have made not the slightest progress of development, and remains very slightly altered since it swam in the waters of the Devonian period. Darwin tells us that "In North America the black bear was seen by Hearne swimming for hours with widely-open mouth, thus catching, like a whale, insects in the water." [How could Hearne tell that insects were the bear's sole object ?] "Even in so extreme a case as this, if the supply of insects were constant, and if better adapted competitors did not exist in the country, I can see no difficulty in a race of bears being rendered by natural selection more and more aquatic in their structure and habits, with larger and larger mouths, till a creature was produced as monstrous as a whale."* The sharks ought surely to have become by this time as monstrous as the whale, with such enlarged advantages of "natural selection." As a rule, however, instead of becoming such monsters, these, as well as all our mammalia, have degenerated in monstrosity from their fossil types. Among the supposed instances of the discovery of the missing link, let us take that of the Simocyonidæ, between the bear and the wolf. It can scarcely be supposed, on any reasonable ground, that the transformation of the extraordinarily active and rapid wolf into the clumsy and slow bear, or *vice versâ*, could have been anything but a slow process, due to some supposed "natural selection," or that the "evolution" was not a gradual one

* "Origin of Species," p. 184.

through ages of time, so that first the long tail disappeared, then the short toes changed to long claws, &c., &c. We should then have every reason to assume that the Simocyonidæ were but a small fraction of the number of links between bear and wolf. But the Darwinian hypothesis assumes that "as all the forms of life are the lineal descendants of those which lived long before the Silurian epoch, we may feel certain that the ordinary succession by generation has never been broken" (p. 489), and as his " long race " of bears at length becoming " monstrous as a whale " requires a lengthy period of gradual changes in structure, so there should be many links between our Simocyonidæ bear and wolf, so ought there to be infinitely more between bear and wolf and their transmutation into horse, stag, elephant, baboon, and man in the "ordinary succession by generation." Here again we rely too much on the "imperfection of the geological record," and might as well interpret that record through the teachings of the open page of Nature of our own epoch, which is utterly silent as to such transmutations; and if we do find similarities or links in greater numbers in the ancient record than among our own fauna, attribute the former with more reason to distinct creations. As we find it a universal law that all genera and species, from man downwards, decline intermixture with other genera and species, so much that even in a state of semi-domestication, or, as I may call it, unnatural selection (the red, for instance, will not even breed with the fallow-deer), all arguments from the attempts of man to create a fusion of species (for such a fusion of genera is well known to be impossible), or to vary their form, are futile, as in the one case the results are hybrids, so that a full stop is put upon the "ordinary succession by generation;" and in the other, all that is done is the production of deformities, which in most cases are not lasting, and which "natural selection," in so far as there is any truth in the doctrine, would certainly cure in time.* For instance, if the bandy-legged deformity of the Ancon sheep, carefully maintained by interbreeding, disappeared with the desire to continue the breed, and supposing that they had been left entirely to Nature, it seems pretty nearly certain that the least bandy-legged and

---

* Huc, in his "Voyage dans le Thibet," vol. ii. p. 221, says, "Les chevaux demi-ânes (cheval hémiane) sont féconds, et se reproduisent en perpétuant l'espèce, qui demeure toujours inaltérable."

consequently more active ram would get the better of the others, and that in the course of time natural operations would reverse the operations of the farmer, and the Ancon race be extinguished. Professor Huxley dilates on the six-fingered individuals of Malta; but what are these but similar monstrosities, like the Ancon sheep or the Siamese twins, the exceptions to the general law of Nature and which Nature is sure to suppress? The extraordinary beak of some pigeons, or additional vertebra, like the occasional sixth finger in man, the Siamese twins, indeed all the so-called varieties reared by man, may be likewise monstrosities which Nature, left to herself, would correct. The question is, what are deformities and what are varieties. Every deviation from the normal type ought perhaps to be considered a deformity, and as such would be corrected to preserve the wonderful order which is exhibited in all nature, and which would be destroyed if monstrosities were allowed to propagate to any great extent. Care may no doubt improve, in our view and for our purposes, races of many animals. We may also be pretty nearly certain that, left to Nature, varieties degenerate (in our view) and revert to their original type. We may also be certain, however, that into whatever varieties closely allied species may change, the animals of different genera will not in any case form alliances in the "ordinary succession by generation." The preservation of favoured races in the struggle for life by means of natural selection, or the converse, but in simpler words, "the weakest go to the wall," may be one of the laws of creation, and to it may be due the preservation of all races in the same forms, and, for thousands of years, even of the same dimensions in which they have hitherto existed, and in such a marvellous and constant order as to enable us to arrange and classify genera and species by the inspection of a single tooth or bone taken from strata of all geological ages. But have we any instance of the destruction in our own age in the struggle for existence of any race or species unless by the act of man? On the contrary, it would seem that, in the wilds of Africa for instance, the Carnivora and Graminivora are so balanced that they do not extirpate one another, and vegetation is supplied, as a rule, equal to their wants. We have no knowledge of the extinction of any genus of our own geological period under the ordinary operations of Nature. That extinction can only be found in former geological periods, and of genera and species essentially differing from those of our geological periods; and as we find new creations, such as the whale and the sheep, surely we may as reasonably suppose new creations of similar though not the same creatures, the general type or model being preserved through all time, as that all should have been evolved from the one, four, or five primordial forms, contrary to all our experience—a conjecture founded upon unnatural (as they may be called) modifications which Nature in time obliterates.

"Geology reveals to us the extraordinary fact, and without its aid the fact never could have been known, that as the globe passed from one condition to another, whole races of animals perished, and were succeeded by others with organizations adapted to the altered state of our planet. On this phenomenon is based the fundamental principle of the identification of strata by their imbedded remains."* But the great mine of the fossil world is very far from being worked out; and therefore, when facts do not fall in conveniently with theories, appeal is made to the imperfection of the geological record, and a serious demand is made upon our credulity, when we are gravely assured of the gradual evolution of all organic creatures from one, or four, or five primordial forms, involving a vast lapse of time and a multiplicity of links, which as yet have not been discovered, notwithstanding their multitude, if they ever existed; for, as to the alleged links, none approach so closely together as our present before-mentioned sirens, snakes, and lizards,

* "Siluria," chap. xliii. p. 1.

of the evolution of which from one another we have not a particle of evidence. If there are such links so closely following in a chain, "the identification of strata by their imbedded remains" would obviously become next to impossible. So satisfactory, however, has been this identification, that it is impossible to ignore it, witness the Silurian strata in all parts of the earth, in which not even a fish has ever been found; also the coal-measures, and indeed all the strata of the earth which are classified or identified by their fossil remains.

The marvellous and constant order in the fauna of the earth is perhaps even more remarkable in the case of its flora. If no single instance of the evolution or transmutation of genera or species of the fauna of the earth has come within our knowledge, still less have we any evidence of the transmutation in a single palpable instance of the trees of the forest or the flowers of the earth; and notwithstanding their endless variety and the myriads of insects carrying the pollen from flower to flower, affording, one would suppose, every facility for transmutation, all remain in their wonderful order, enabling us, as in the case of the fauna, to classify and arrange. Dr. Hooker has indeed suggested conspicuous examples of unstable forms and apparent transitional links, which one would suppose might only be varieties. Professor Parrot shows one of the modes by which these changes in plants may be accounted for; there are probably many others. "These changes in plants, resulting from the height of situation, were first observed by me during my travels in the Caucasus, on which occasion I accurately described them. I subsequently made the same observations on the Swiss and Italian Alps, and on the Pyrenees, and now they were again repeated in the most unequivocal manner on Ararat: so that several different kinds of plants occur equally under the same circumstances on all those mountains, the several specimens coinciding most completely; whereas they have so little resemblance to the very same plants growing in the lower regions of the same mountain tract that one would hardly suspect them to be of the same species."* Surely, if we seek for laws, we must find them in the immense multitude of examples which are visibly constant and invariable, and certainly not dogmatize on a few possibly, nay, probably, only apparent exceptions.

* "Journey to Ararat," by Dr. F. Parrot, Cooley's translation, p. 201.

Let us imagine the destruction of the present external crust of the earth, and, like the different geological periods—primary, secondary, and tertiary—a new geological period, only distinguishable by its imbedded fossil remains, the remains of all our living creatures, including man, and, with him, his works. Let us also imagine a new or remodelled earth's surface, and a new race of intellectual reasoning animals like ourselves. Now suppose philosophers of this new state of things discovering the fossils of the horse (*Equus curvidens*) of America, and finding above them, in the strata of our period, the fossils of the horse of our period. Some of these philosophers would contend, very naturally but very untruly, that the horse of our day was the descendant of *Equus curvidens* in the "ordinary succession by generation," for the American horse of our day was introduced by the Spaniards into that continent, nor was any such animal known to exist there previously to that introduction. If, therefore, such a mistake might so easily be made in the case of species so closely allied, we may with more reason infer that it is a gross mistake to suppose the evolution of one distinct genus from another by the " ordinary succession by generation." Again, the same philosophers of the supposed new period would find the casts of anchors of every variety of form in the rocks or deposits of only the former strata, some very rude, some of very perfect shapes, or of fragments of boats and ships of an immense variety, but a variety which still showed them to have, in one sense, a common origin; that is to say, to have been the creation of some intelligent being.

In the same way we see the creations of an infinitely higher intelligence, and have no more reason to conclude the evolution contrary to all experience of one from the other, than in the case of the anchor or the ship. The beautiful little anchors which cover the body of the Synapta, and from which the idea of one of our patent anchors would seem to have been taken, compared as to their origin with our anchors, may afford instruction to those who cannot comprehend a supreme creative intelligence beyond that of man. Perhaps if, following the reasoning of some of our scientific men, the suggested philosopher of a new period of the earth's crust might pronounce these minute anchors, which he should find in a fossil state, the germs or the primordial form of all the fossil anchors.

It is alleged that some of the well-known

facts of comparative anatomy, as for instance the foot of marsupials, are inexplicable on any other theory but that of evolution. Many natural facts were inexplicable to former philosophers, except through theories long since exploded. This theory seems to be of the same character, and is constructed upon a few, as yet, inexplicable facts (if indeed it be true that they are not explicable on the theory of distinct creation), in the teeth of the universal law which has preserved genera and species for thousands of years in precisely the same forms and with the same anatomical distinctions as they present themselves to us to this day.

Mr. Darwin's final conclusion, that mankind is descended from an ape-like progenitor in the ordinary succession by generation from some of the monkey tribes, the pointed ears, tail, &c., being at last obliterated but leaving their traces, seems to contradict his principle of "natural selection" and the doctrine of the "survival of the fittest." Since reading his book, I have been in the habit of looking at human ears, and as far as I have seen, the point in the ear on which he partly founds his conclusion is completely absent; as for the tail, no human beings have as yet been found with that accommodation, not even as an exceptional deformity, great as the advantage would have been of a prehensile one, especially to sailors.

We are told that in the "struggle for existence" the weaker animal must give way to the stronger, and the weaker be extinguished or absorbed in the stronger race. Now man is physically the least fitted animal to contend in that struggle with others, not being furnished, as all other animals, with offensive or defensive organs, and with less physical strength than the anthromorphous apes, man's nearest congeners; consequently, unless all the imaginary Simian progenitors produced a new creature, mentally though not physically superior, at one and the same time (not very probable), this half-man half-ape would infallibly fail in the "struggle for existence." A single man-eating tiger will even now compel a whole village in India to migrate; how much more would the powerful gorilla or ourang outang make mincemeat of some feeble link or links between themselves and man! Sir Charles Lyell alludes to this difficulty, the feebleness of man as compared with animals, and says, "But this difficulty has been met, as before stated, by assigning as the original seat of man, some island within

the tropics free from large beasts of prey."*
This conjecture, to meet the difficulties of
another conjecture, seems to involve a contradiction of the doctrine of "progressive
development in the struggle for existence."
Surely the weak animal, half-man half-ape,
would have little chance in his island in the
struggle for existence with his powerful
relations, gorilla or ourang. The fruits of the
trees would be seized before he could reach
them, and he would be pushed aside in the
struggle for the fruits of the ground, and
therefore have small chance of progressive
development. Surrounded by water, the
ourang's half-developed progeny might doubtless have been driven out of its tropical island,
and obliged to find a refuge on a neighbouring
continent, which implies either swimming, for

* "Principles," p. 466.

which the Simian race are not remarkable, or the power of constructing something in the nature of raft or boat, or drifting on a log with a very moderate distance of water to cross; but on the continent they would have found as dangerous enemies to progress as in their tropical island-home, in the tropical lion, tiger, &c. All history and tradition are against the conjecture, and the tradition—no ordinary one—of the garden of Eden seems a far more rational solution of the problem. Why the gorilla, or ourang, or other baboon should have ceased, in their undisturbed forests, whether island or continental, to produce their superior congener, man, or at least some kind of half-breed, for so many thousand years, and should only have done so in the Miocene or Pleiocene period, conjecturers must further determine. Why the ourang or gorilla, with all the advantages of seclusion in impenetrable jungles or forests, with habits formed, in some cases, of building (in which, however, they are by no means as proficient as birds), should not have become monstrous in intelligence, as the bear, swimming about with open mouth, in magnitude, and produced by progressive development, in the last few centuries of the millions of years they are supposed to have existed, a single palpable link between themselves and man, one is at a loss to conceive.

Millions upon millions of suns, and probably planets, are recognised facts; so are millions of miles of space. Millions of years are unhesitatingly admitted by many philosophers into calculations of the time required for the formation of portions of the earth's crust; why should they have any difficulty in admitting and believing in thousands, or even millions, of created organic beings, or their germs, protoplasms, or primordial forms, when they see the infinite millions of created things in the heavens, including, probably, infinite millions more which they do not see?

Mr. Darwin's new theory of "sexual selection" is introduced as another mode of natural selection in the struggle for existence, and is based upon the assumption that in some cases the female selects the male, not the male the female; for it is unquestionable that with respect to the mammalia the male selects, as he acknowledges in the case of the seal, and as is well known in the case of the stag, the bull, the buffalo, &c. In the semi-wild herds of buffaloes in Italy, after a contest between the bulls for the females, the conquered bull retires to some thicket in a state of insanity, and from thence rushes out at and kills every living thing that passes. Sportsmen are warned to take care of the "bufalo matto" by the peasants, and very dangerous it is to fall in with one. It is also assumed that birds have an æsthetic taste for beauty; may they not in that case have other tastes, for a good-tempered male for instance, independent of his beauty? Then again, does the improvement of the race depend upon the male alone; has not the health and strength, and perhaps beauty of the female, something to do with her offspring?

"The males, as we have seen, are generally ready to breed before the females; of the males the strongest, and, with some species, the best armed, drive away the weaker males, and the former would then unite with the more vigorous and best-nourished females, as these are the first to breed. Such vigorous pairs would surely rear a larger number of offspring than the retarded females, which would be compelled, supposing the sexes to be numerically equal, to unite with the conquered and less powerful males; and this is all that is wanted to add, in the course of successive generations, to the size, strength, and courage of the males, or to improve their weapons."* According to this statement of the case, it would seem that even these male birds *select* the "more vigorous and best-nourished females."

This supposed improvement by sexual selection, doubtful at the best, and founded upon one class of animal life, to the exclusion of the opposite evidence afforded by the mammalia, is adduced as proof of the

* "The Descent of Man," vol. i. p. 261.

supposed law which affects all organic beings; but as we have been acquainted with many animals, through the records of past ages of one kind or other for thousands of years, surely we ought to find evidence of their improvement in "size and strength," and an improvement of their weapons. Such, however, is notoriously not the case. And if we take the instance, among others, of the peacock, we may see the portrait of our present peacock, exactly as he is now, as well as of other animals, in the ancient monuments of Rome, Egypt and Nineveh.

If it be true that, through "natural selection" and the "struggle for existence, the stronger and generally improved individuals of every species have been gradually improving the race and adding to their strength, size, and courage," and the improvement of their weapons, it follows that the present species must be superior to their ancient progenitors, or, conversely, that the ancient progenitors must have been inferior in strength and size, and courage, and with inferior weapons; but if the present species of the earth are, as asserted, the descendants of those we find in a fossil state, the very reverse is the case, for the fossils of almost all species show that they were very much superior in size, strength, and with much more powerful weapons. Witness the saurians, and nearly all the mammalia. The theory, therefore, of sexual selection is founded upon a very questionable, not to say false, basis, being directly contradicted in many instances by our own experience of some thousand years. The true law seems to be that the strongest male, whether more or less perfect or beautiful (admitting that beauty is a proof of the stronger and more perfect animal), will to a certain extent exclude the less powerful male, thus preserving the race in the same form and condition through ages, and preventing its deterioration and annihilation, rather than causing future progressive development of any kind in ages to come, for which progressive development in the past we have not a particle of evidence.

PROFESSOR HUXLEY ON DARWINISM.

PROFESSOR HUXLEY, in his "Lay Sermons on the Origin of Species," takes the opportunity of heaping eulogistic phrases upon science in general and invention, and contempt upon those who differ in opinion from Mr. Darwin, although he himself is but a half-and-half believer; they are "pietists," "bibliolaters," "bigots," "old ladies of both sexes," &c. Abuse and ridicule are calculated to inflict pain—a kind of persecution which Professor Huxley deprecates very properly as applied to scientific men of former days; and it is to be hoped that he will condescend to approve and observe the sacred maxim, "Do unto others as you wish they should do unto you."

"The coeval imaginations," he says,* "current among the rude inhabitants of Palestine, recorded by writers whose very name and age are admitted by every scholar to be unknown, have not yet shared their fate [the myths of paganism], but even at this day are regarded by nine-tenths of the civilised world as the authoritative standard of fact, and the criterion of the justice of scientific conclusions in all that relates to the origin of things, and, among these, of species." And again, sarcastically, "The first chapter of Genesis contains the beginning and end of sound science."

Nine-tenths of the civilised world! Are

* "Lay Sermons," &c., p. 305.

they all "pietists," "bigots," "old ladies of both sexes," &c.? At all events they are in the scientific good company of Bacon, Newton, and Faraday—men as scientific as any of our present professors of science. Huxley's statement of their opinions is a most unfair one. They do not expect to find in the few brief and majestic words of the first chapter of Genesis a scientific exposition, they find there the most concise account of an event which it would take a library of books to explain in detail. They hold its authenticity upon far better and sounder evidence than is produced for the conjectures of Lamarck and Darwin; and if, on account of the want of the name and age of the writers or writer, compilers or annalists of this book of a remote antiquity, authenticated as it has been by other histories, monuments, &c., together with other more remarkable evidences of its truth, it is not to be believed, we may as well shut up all history, which always must consist of compilations from other writers. The name of the author of any history is no criterion of its greater or less credibility, except perhaps to his cotemporaries. No one but an inspired person could give a true authoritative account of Creation, and happily for the good of mankind, nine-tenths of the civilised world are satisfied that the author of Genesis was so inspired; but to say that they regard it as the criterion of the justice of scientific conclusions, that the first chapter of Genesis contains the beginning and end of sound science, is a very deceptive statement of the views of "nine-tenths of the civilised world." The great truth taught by the first chapter of Genesis, that the Almighty God was the

Creator of heaven and earth, may, in one sense, be held by the nine-tenths, including some of the greatest of the wise and the scientific, as the "beginning and end of sound science;" but that so concise a narrative of such a stupendous work as that of the creation of a world could possibly give us any insight into the *modus operandi* of "the mystery of mysteries, Creation," as Darwin justly calls it, they, I imagine, do not believe and cannot regard it as the criterion of the justice of particular so-called scientific conclusions. It must not be forgotten that the great truth of the one God, the Creator of all things, was preserved to the world by the "semi-barbarous" Jewish people alone, in the midst of the general idolatry of surrounding nations, in probably the only form in which that nation and myriads of the unscientific could understand it, leaving to the scientific—the drops in the ocean of humanity—a large field for speculation and conjecture as to the process of Creation. Darwin, vol. i. p. 182, says, "The highest form of religion—the grand idea of God hating sin and loving righteousness—was unknown in primæval times." It was certainly not unknown in the primæval times of the history of the Bible, the only ones of which we have any knowledge. Surely the ten Commandments, the formulated expression of the sentiments expressed throughout in the Bible in the primæval times, before the promulgation of the Commandments, show the knowledge of a "God hating sin and loving righteousness."

The Professor asserts that "The doctrine of special creation owes its existence to the supposed necessity of making science accord with the Hebrew cosmogony; but it is curious to observe that, as the doctrine is at present maintained, it is as hopelessly inconsistent with the Hebrew view as any other hypothesis."

The Mosaic account of Creation, as before suggested, is manifestly a popular, as it may be called, and not a scientific account, for the best of reasons, that if clothed in a scientific form it would have been wholly unintelligible to the great mass of its readers; we cannot therefore expect to deduce from it any arguments as to the *modus operandi* of Creation. Whatever, therefore, may be the doctrine of special creation as maintained *at present* by some men of science, others may be permitted to hold the view that it is not inconsistent with Hebrew cosmogony, especially since there are so many professors and others holding such different views on many a scientific question, involved in the attempt to construct a cosmogony. An authoritative revelation of the one Almighty Creator of the universe to his intelligent creatures appears to have been necessary to control the vagaries of human reason. Montaigne has described those of the ancient philosophers, and amusingly winds up his account:—"Fiez-vous à vostre philosophie; vantez-vous d'avoir trouvé la febve au gasteau, à veoir ce tintamarre de tant de cervelles philosophiques." *

In their various attempts at the construction of theories to explain the mode of creation of the globe, and things upon it, modern "scientific men" are not unlikely to find a commentator like Montaigne. One of the last of these theories supposes meteoric stones,

* "Œuvres de Montaigne," J. A. Buchon, p. 280.

usually, if not always, of some metallic substance in an incandescent state, to have contained and supplied the seeds or germs of the growths with which the earth is filled.

The only certain *scientific* conclusion at which we can arrive through that chapter of Genesis, is that God was the Creator of all things, and that the conjecture of "the fool who has said in his heart there is no God," that some fortuitous combination of molecular forces has developed into the wonderful order and harmony of the universe, is nonsense. With those holding decided views of progressive development, it seems extraordinary that there should be any difficulty in believing that man is not the end and summit of intellectual existence, and that there should not be improved existences, or existences of another nature, good and bad, not so intimately connected with earthy matter as we are. If "man is developed from an ovule, about the 125th of an inch diameter,"* a microscopic object, perhaps in an earlier stage even more minute, developed into the form of intellectual man, it seems reasonable to infer that after death the vital energy may still remain in some minute germ or ovule, be developed into, or as St. Paul says, "raised a spiritual body," or clothed in another form of matter, and man thereby given "hopes for a still higher destiny in the distant future;"* not, as I suppose Mr. Darwin means, an improved animal on this earth, or merely an improvement of the race, which to each of us individually would be, instead of a hope, a painful regret that we cannot expect to

* "Descent of Man," vol. i. p. 14.
† Ibid., vol. ii. p. 405.

participate in the improvement, but a hope in which each individual man is concerned personally, of which some of our modern "scientific conclusions" would fain deprive us, and of which Mr. Darwin's conclusions will assuredly not deprive many "of the nine-tenths of the civilised world."

Well may we more than admire the beautiful ancient symbol of a future glorified existence—the butterfly; the creeping caterpillars finishing their existence in their coffin, the chrysalis, and finally emerging from it, in some cases, in the most gorgeous forms in Nature. Nor should we forget that the germ of the caterpillar must contain in some wonderful manner the essence or substance which is elaborated into the exceeding beauty of the butterfly. How is it possible to explain this marvellous metamorphosis? and knowing, seeing it, why have the smallest doubt of the authoritatively-declared metamorphosis of the intellectual being, man?

"When astronomy was young," the morning stars sang together for joy, "and the planets were guided in their courses by celestial hands. Now the harmony of the stars has resolved itself into gravitation according to the inverse square of their distances, and the orbits of the planets are deducible from the laws of the forces which allow a schoolboy's stone to break a window. The lightning was the Angel of the Lord; but it has pleased Providence in these modern times that science should make it the humble messenger of man."* Here, by the way, the Professor uses a figure much like that of the Bible. Electricity, not *lightning*, has

---

* "Lay Sermons," &c., p. 310.

been made the humble messenger of man. Lightning still remains, not the humble messenger, but too often the irresistible destroyer of man.

It is a subject of regret to find a professor treating a matter so interesting and serious to nine-tenths of the civilised world in a manner so scornful and so shallow. To quote a poetical expression from a poetical work (the Book of Job), as a scientific exposition of a natural fact, and then to draw an invidious comparison between it and the prose of a geometrical law, when, moreover, there are many passages elsewhere in the Bible showing that the writers held no such unscientific notions, certainly does not betray much regard for fairness and truth. Where the Professor finds that the lightning was "the Angel of the Lord," I am at a loss to discover, unless he confounds the φλόγα πυρὸς, "flame of fire," the figurative words of St. Paul, taken from the poetical language of the 104th Psalm, with ἀστραπή, "lightning." As well might he accuse Goethe of a want of astronomical knowledge for writing in the opening of "Faust," "Die Sönne tönt nach alter Weise in Brüder-sphären Wettgesang." If this be a specimen of scientific liberalism on which he prides himself, scientific liberalism will with reason stink in the nostrils of "nine-tenths of the civilised world." To show no respect for the opinions of these nine-tenths, and insult them with opprobrious terms, is that kind of liberalism which is so remarkable in the Bradlaughs and Odgers of the present day.

Professor Huxley says, "A section, a hundred feet thick, will exhibit at different heights a dozen species of ammonite, none of which passes beyond its particular zone of limestone or clay into the zone below it or into that above it; so that those who adopt the doctrine of special creation, must be prepared to admit that at intervals of time corresponding with the thickness of those beds, the Creator thought fit to interfere with the natural course of events for the purpose of making a new ammonite."* What can the Professor know of the "natural course of events" in the ammonite world? In that presumptuous certainty of the correctness of his inductions he seems to think he has triumphantly posed the believer in special creation; but Dr. Carpenter's researches in the deep sea have shown the foolishness of those inductions, and that different creatures simultaneously

* "Lay Sermons," p. 308.

exist in zones of different heights, and that the "*intervals of time* corresponding with the thickness of these beds" may be *no intervals at all.* Why should not the Creator have thought fit to create varieties of ammonites as well as the infinite varieties in all Nature, an infinite variety extending throughout the universe, if Mr. Proctor, in his lecture, Royal Institution, May 6, 1870, is correct in saying that the chief characteristic of the sidereal system is its infinite variety.

After this nullification of the Professor's scientific sarcasm, we may laugh at his additional remark: "But the hypothesis of special creation is not only a mere specious mask for our ignorance, its existence in biology marks the youth and imperfection of the science."*

He uses also the phrase, "Force the

* "Lay Sermons," p. 310.

generous new wine of science into the old bottles of Judaism." The discoveries of Dr. Carpenter have turned some of this generous wine very sour.

At page 74 of his "Lay Sermons," he lays down some excellent rules for the instruction of the young in science, but on a sudden we come to the very startling recommendation or instruction, "and especially tell him [a child!] that it is his duty to doubt until he is compelled by the absolute authority of Nature to believe that which is written in books." Following such astounding and mischievous advice, the child would believe nothing beyond that which it discovers by its own personal experience, and certainly not the "Lay Sermons." This, indeed, would not be an unmitigated evil. The misstatements of facts, lies, false-reasoning from doubtful facts and conclusions, false "deductions, inductions, and ratiocinations," are so commonly "written in books," that it is not extraordinary that some men should drop into the folly of a universal scepticism, and especially in scientific questions, as they observe so often "scientific men" holding diametrically opposite opinions before commissions, committees of the House of Commons, and in courts of law engaged in such questions. "What is truth?" they ask. The Professor's advice would tend to increase this scepticism; which, however, men contrive somehow or other to forget in the thousand and one concerns of their daily life.

But the fact is that men, let alone children, as far as the knowledge of Nature, or indeed any kind of knowledge, is concerned, must to a great extent be as grown children as far as belief in "that which is written in books;"

for few, we may say none, have the time or the opportunity for an appeal to the "absolute authority of Nature," or in other words, to experiment or direct observation of all the multitudinous varieties of Nature's operations. One can understand a professor of anatomy saying to his pupils, "Do not take for granted what I tell you or what you read, but test the truth for yourself as you have the means of testing it;" but to lay down the same principle for children generally seems positively mischievous, and it is to be hoped will not be an instruction of the Board of Education. Teachers will not stand being told by children that they do not believe them, and I pity the child who adopts the Professor's scientific doctrine. As Carlyle tersely puts it —the clerk in Eastcheap cannot be for ever verifying his ready-reckoner.

In almost every concern of life we are compelled to have more or less faith or belief in what we read or are told by others. "Ne sutor ultra crepidam" is a valuable maxim. Everybody cannot know everything. We must therefore rely upon or have faith in others. It is a necessity of our nature, and must extend from very many of the lowest to the very highest consideration. The man or child would be an incredulous fool who refused to believe anything for which he could not obtain "the absolute authority of Nature." How the Professor, requiring a child to have the "*absolute* authority of Nature" for his belief, can subscribe the Darwinian doctrine, seems very extraordinary, as that doctrine certainly has not that *absolute* authority.

"The species of animals which inhabit the

opposite sides of the Isthmus of Panama are wholly distinct, &c.; but where the student seeks an explanation of them from the supporters of the received hypothesis of the origin of species, the reply he receives is, in substance, of Oriental simplicity, 'Mashallah, it so pleased God.' There are different species on opposite sides of the Isthmus of Panama, because they were created different on the two sides," &c.* In another place Professor Huxley writes:—"All who are confident to express an opinion are, at present, agreed that the manifold varieties of animal and vegetable form have not come into existence by chance, nor result from capricious exertion of creative power."†

We find also in Fritz Müller's "Facts and Arguments for Darwin," p. 22:—"To the old

* "Lay Sermons," p. 312. † Ibid., p. 236.

school, this occurrence of two kinds of males [of the *Taxcis dubius*], a microscopic isopod, will appear to be merely a matter of curiosity. To those who regard the 'plan of Creation' as the conception of an Almighty intellect, matured in the thoughts of the latter before it is manifested in palpable external forms, it will appear a mere *caprice* of the Creator, as it is inexplicable either from the points of view of practical adaptation or from the typical plan of structure. From the side of Darwin's theory this fact acquires meaning and significance." It would doubtless appear to the old school, and to every one else, a matter not "merely," but very remarkably, a matter of curiosity; but the idea of mere caprice of the Creator seems a puerile objection to the doctrine of special creation; for supposing that all genera and species have sprung from a "germ" or "protoplasm," or the "one primordial form into which life was first breathed by the Creator," or the four or five of Darwin, is it to be supposed for one moment that He who created that germ, protoplasm, or primordial form, was not aware beforehand of the infinite varieties of form which it would assume? The absurd notion of *caprice* might therefore as unreasonably be entertained by the follower of Darwin as by any other inventor of theories. What can we pretend to know of the "practical adaptation" of certain relations of the microscopic isopod, or whether even the two males may not be according to *typical plan of structure* in other microscopic isopods with which we are so little acquainted? This is going very far to fetch an argument for Darwinism, which one would suppose, according to "sexual selection," would decree the destruction of the weaker male.

The creations of mankind are faint images of the creations of God. The Greeks and Etruscans have left us a great variety of beautiful forms in their pottery. Do we call this caprice? Would not one identical form of pot have answered all the purpose? Is it caprice which has dictated all the endless varieties of form of the useful and the ornamental of man's creation? For what object the infinite, wonderful, and beautiful varieties of God's creation should have been placed on this earth at all, who can pretend to explain? We are compelled to say, "Mashallah, it so pleased God."

Professor Huxley again says: *—"The 'special creation' hypothesis presumes every

* "Lay Sermons," &c., p. 306.

species to have originated from one or more stocks, these not being the result of any other form of living matter, or arising by natural agencies, but being produced, as such, by a supernatural creative act." Happily the Professor does not entertain the view that the varieties of animal or vegetable life have come into existence by chance, or that inert matter can have by its inert self produced the wonderful harmony, adaptation to purpose, extraordinary combinations of mechanical and other laws, and the mysterious energies of life. We will leave that to the "fool who has said in his heart there is no God." But it seems more easy to believe in the "supernatural creative act" of some hundreds or thousands of genera and species as of the one or four or five of Darwin, into which "life," as he says, "was first breathed by the Creator," than in the creation of one or more eozoons, which should expand into the multitudes of organic life. It is contrary to the experience of some thousands of years, that any single genus has, "in the ordinary succession by generation," ever diverged into any other form, or that any species has undergone any other change but a slight modification, under exceptional circumstances, and with a large amount of evidence in most cases that a return to normal circumstances will restore the species to its normal form.

Again, he says "the 'transmutation' hypothesis considers that all existing species are the result of the modification of pre-existing species, and those of their predecessors by agencies similar to those which at the present day produce varieties and races, and therefore is altogether a natural way; and it is probable, though not a necessary consequence of this hypothesis, that all living beings have arisen from a single stock." This hypothesis then supposes a modification of species such as those of our own days into varieties of races and species, not of genera as well as species, which is the Darwinian theory, and of which we have no knowledge or experience at the present or at any other time whatever, and, as we have said before, these so-called varieties and races have naturally a tendency to revert to their original forms rather than to perpetuate their variations.

So uncertain, so impalpable a hypothesis, so mysterious this problem of creation and life, that it seems mere dogmatism to insist upon the truth of such theories, and an unwholesome return to the anti-Baconian days of scientific reasoning.

"Huxley is doing his best to back up Darwin," says Sir Wm. Denison.* "What I have seized upon is his admission that the brain of the gorilla is *as perfect* as that of man. If this be the case, the inference is simple, that the brain which in its perfect state allows a brute to be *such a brute* cannot be that which constitutes a man." Darwin would perhaps reply that natural or sexual selection has effected the improvement which constitutes the human brain at some remote period; but why this improvement should not have continued, and have been constantly going on with men and monkeys, remains to be explained. Cuvier's doctrine would appear far more rational:—"Le développement des êtres organisés est plus ou moins prompt et plus ou moins étendus, selon que

* "Varieties of Viceregal Life," vol. ii. p. 230.

les circonstances lui sont plus ou moins favorable. La chaleur, l'abondance, et l'espèce de la nourriture, d'autres causes encore y influent, et cette influence peut être générale sur tout le corps, ou partielle sur certaines organes; de là vient que la similitude des descendans avec leurs parents ne peut jamais être parfaite. Les différences de ce genre, entre les êtres organisés, sont ce qu'on appelle des variétés. On n'a aucune preuve que toutes les différences qui distinguent aujourd'hui les êtres organisés soient de nature à avoir pu être ainsi produites par les circonstances. Tout ce que l'on a avancé sur ce sujet est hypothétique; l'expérience paraît montrer au contraire que, dans l'état actuel du globe, les variétés sont renfermées dans des limites assez étroites, et, aussi loin que nous pouvons remonter dans l'antiquité, nous voyons que ces limites étaient les mêmes qu'aujourd'hui. On est donc obligé d'admettre certaines formes, qui se sont perpétués depuis l'origine des choses sans excéder ses limites ; et tout les êtres appartenant à l'une de ces formes constituent ce que l'on appelle une *espèce*. Les variétés sont des subdivisions accidentelles de l'espèce."*

"It is notorious that man is constructed on the same general type or model with other mammals," † it is, therefore, not surprising "that their tissues and blood" should have a similarity to those of lower animals. "Monkeys are liable to many of the same non-contagious diseases as we are"—"the *Cebus Azaræ*, in its native land," ‡ is found liable to catarrh. But so is the dog and

---

* "Règne Animal," p. 19.
† "Descent of Man," vol. i. p. 10.   ‡ Ibid., p. 11.

horse, also from apoplexy, &c., as well as monkeys. Medicine also produces the same or a similar effect on other animals besides monkeys. Horses will drink beer in Germany, as well as monkeys brandy; but I do not know whether any other animals but monkeys have been taught to smoke, except perhaps the dog. In short, in his material internal as well as external form, man "is constructed on the same general type or model" with other mammals, and as these have been constructed in a gradation of resemblances of one kind or another, the last gradation the nearest in the scale to man is no doubt the monkey. Upon these resemblances the theory of Mr. Darwin has apparently been formed—a theory, or rather conjecture, founded upon most uncertain evidence, which must be for ever wanting in logical proof; and why it should cease to operate, why one mammal should not be evolving new forms, and the ourang or gorilla producing ape-like men or some other "hairy quadruped furnished with a tail and pointed ears," or why no fossil trace has been found of any one of the "series of forms graduating insensibly from some ape-like creature, to man as he now exists,"* though the monkey has been found fossil in Miocene strata, seems very surprising if there be a shadow of truth in the theory. On the contrary, it seems much more probable that creation has completed the series as it now exists and from which it never varies, the supposed missing links between the monkey and man, the imaginary "hairy quadruped," being as mythical as the faun, centaur, merman and mermaid of former

* "Descent of Man," vol. i. p. 233.

days. There are, however, genera or species more or less closely resembling one another, and some apparent links between them, such, for instance, as between the snake and the lizard; for we have, as mentioned before, the little sirens, some with two, some with four little legs, with different numbers of toes, and the carpet snake of Australia.* Here we have closely apparent links between snake or lizard; but what is this, but only a closer adherence to similarity of type or model in these particular instances. They are, however, specifically distinct, and I presume no one will pretend that snake or lizard *evolves* sirens, or *vice versâ*, or to explain why, if ever there were such evolution, that evolution is not still in progress before our eyes. This instance of

* These four-legged little snakes swarm in parts of the Roman Campagna in the spring season.

a close similarity of form in living creatures of one genus ought to raise a very substantial doubt of the truth of transmutation or evolution theories, or of the gradual and progressive development of man from an ape-like progenitor through many forms, even if we were to discover any of these supposed fossil links or forms which are now so conspicuously wanting.

In Knightley's "The Hermits," p. 87, we find that St. Anthony "sees in a stony valley a short manikin, with crooked nose and brow rough with horns, whose lower parts ended in goat's feet," and Anthony, "asking him who he was, was answered, I am a mortal, and one of the inhabitants of the desert, whom the Gentiles, deluded by various errors, worship by the name of fauns, satyrs, and incubi." According to Darwin, this story ought to be considered credible; and St. Jerome adds, p. 88, "Lest this should move a scruple in any one on account of its incredibility, it was corroborated, in the reign of Constantine, by the testimony of the whole world. For a man of that kind, being led alive to Alexandria, afforded a great spectacle to the people; and afterwards the lifeless carcass, being salted lest it should decay in the summer heat, was brought to Antioch, to be seen by the Emperor."

Having been assured by an eminent lawyer that he had seen a child with the legs of a moose deer, which had frightened the mother of the child before her confinement, St. Jerome's fact may possibly be credible, and the strange animal not a clever deception; but the inference from it is not tenable. Such monstrosities, like the Siamese twins, &c., are possible. Mr. Darwin's theory would justify

St. Jerome in his belief to the fullest extent, and his followers may perhaps welcome this creature of St. Anthony's as one of the missing links.

Professor Huxley says, "The solvency of great mercantile companies rests on the validity of the laws which have been ascertained to govern the seeming irregularity of that human life, which the moralist bewails as the most uncertain of things; plague, pestilence, and famine are admitted, by all but fools, to be the natural result of causes for the most part fully within human control, and not the unavoidable tortures inflicted by wrathful Omnipotence upon his helpless handiwork."*

Is it possible that the Professor means to take the moralist to task, and will assure the certainty of his own life for the next three,

* "Lay Sermons," p. 311.

seven, or twenty-one years, as he would the lease of a house, upon the validity of this so-called law, by which life assurance companies are enabled to run the risks of the uncertainty of life? It is found from certain tables of mortality, experience, and calculations founded upon them, that, taking a large number of persons in good health at various periods of life, the chances of the duration of life are for so many years, and allowing a good margin for the uncertainty, the insurance companies stake the certainty of their capital and a large amount in premiums (and nothing but a large number of premiums can give any chance of success) against the uncertainty of life; which, however, notwithstanding all this care in selection, inquiry, and medical investigation, they have often to bewail with "the moralist," as too many modern companies know to their cost.

The "fools" would be much obliged to the wise men of science if they would show them how to put seasons of excessive drought, or of excessive rain and snow, heat and cold, the epidemics which attack vegetation and animals—the potatoe disease for instance—the cholera, yellow fever, and the variety of pestilences which have swept over the earth, under human control. They come and they depart, a scourge to the organic beings of the world; and all that man can do, scarcely even "for the most part," and by no means "fully," is to mitigate in some cases their severity. As far as man is concerned, some epidemics may be mitigated, it is doubtful whether they could be averted, by sanitary measures. But decay and death is part of the order of all creation on this earth, and in the case of mankind, is more or less preceeded by sufferings, diseases, or accidents, which are in a multiplicity of cases not "within human control," and we seem to be as far as ever from the time when the soul shall leave the body without such antecedent sufferings, all the men of science notwithstanding. They are tortures inflicted upon the helpless handiwork of the Creator; but we have no right to say they are inflicted by "wrathful Omnipotence," any more than the ignorant or stupid man would have to say that the punishment of death or imprisonment, involving probably mental torture quite equivalent to physical pain, was the wrathful act of a government; for we are in complete ignorance of the reason why Omnipotence has thought fit to allow the existence of pain and death, and of evil, their fruitful cause; and in that ignorance we must remain, for we never can expect to understand the great scheme of the universe, or solve the mystery of the existence and the origin of evil.

This painful part of the law of existence must for the present be part of the great scheme; but, none the less, this physical law may be closely connected with the moral law. Sir Charles Bell, one of our truest experimental philosophers, says, "But why then have I such inexhaustible delight in the whole face of Nature? No, it is the pleasure I have in investigating structure. Everything there so perfect, so curiously fitted, and leading you by little and little to the comprehension of a wisdom so perfect that I am forced to believe that, in the moral world things are not really left in all that disarray which our partial view would persuade us they are."*

* "Letters of Sir C. Bell," p. 251.

The Bible, however, supplies a consolation for sufferers, and the manner in which the apparent "disarray" is provided for. To cite one of many such comforting assurances, St. Paul, referring to the fact of the existence of evil, "the world groaneth and travaileth with pain until now,"* shows them a glorious compensation in the hope of happiness in a future life, and not on very severe conditions, many of which consist of means of making life in this world less miserable. Who even in this life would not willingly submit to a few months or years of suffering, for the prospect of the enjoyment of a long life of health? In fact, men are ready to undergo the pain of a fearful operation for the sake of a prospective, even uncertain, cure. Of this hope of happiness in a future life some men of

* Romans viii.

science are striving to deprive mankind — a boon perhaps to the worst portion of our race, who contribute so largely to its miseries, by relieving them of the fear of forfeiture of that hope and of the punishment of their crimes.

If in the foregoing extract the Professor only means that we have no right to assume that any special infliction is the punishment of Heaven for any special iniquity, he will be only repeating the teaching of Christ, who said, "He maketh his sun to rise on the evil and the good, and sendeth the rain on the just and on the unjust."* The parable of the tares,† and the reference to the Galileans, whose blood Pilate had mingled with their sacrifices, and the eighteen upon whom the tower of Siloam fell,‡ show also that we have no right as Christians to assume that cala-

* Matthew v. 45.   † Ib. xiii.   ‡ Luke xiii.

mities are necessarily punishments inflicted by the Creator in this world; and yet at the same time it does not follow that there may not be exceptions to the rule, and that great natural disasters may be punishments specially inflicted for great moral crime, though nothing but inspired authority would justify us in asserting them to be so in particular instances.

It is difficult to understand the value of a remark that Mr. Darwin and Mr. Wallace have done good to science by making people think. As well might it be said that the invention of a number of falsehoods did good, by bringing out the truth. Or again, that science cannot make progress without theorizers. It seems a question whether theorizers, who produce theories based upon false or very uncertain grounds, do not rather injure than benefit the cause of true science, by lowering it as well as its professors in the estimation of the world in general.

Professor Huxley, referring to the teleogical argument, says*—"The teleogical argument runs thus: an organ or organism (A) is precisely fitted to perform a function or purpose (B), therefore it was specially constructed to perform that function;" and at page 332, "Far from imagining that cats exist *in order* to catch mice well, Darwinism supposes that cats exist because they catch mice well—mousing being not the end, but the condition of their existence." It will hardly be denied that the stomach of the cat was "precisely fitted to perform a function," that of assimilating and digesting its food; then it would follow that its claws, teeth, and admirable agility, "were precisely fitted" to fill that stomach, or, in

* "Lay Sermons," &c., p. 330.

other words, to catch its prey—rats, mice, birds and such small deer,—and, to go a little further, that its rough tongue was "precisely fitted" to enable it to work up the flesh and skin of the animals it destroys, as the lion's tongue is armed with a formidable array of hooked bones for a like purpose. But for what purpose the tail of the cat, if not to give (it is but a suggestion) expressive signs of its different mental emotions? Mr. Darwin, in the "Origin of Species," p. 196, gives us the following theory on the tail generally,—"Seeing how important an organ of locomotion the tail is in most aquatic animals, its general presence and use for so many land animals, which in their lungs and modified air-bladders betray their aquatic origin, may perhaps be thus accounted for. A well-developed tail having been formed in an aquatic animal, it might subsequently come to be worked in for all sorts of purposes, as a fly-flapper, an organ of prehension, or as an aid in turning, as with the dog, though the aid must be slight, for the hare, with hardly any tail, can double quickly enough." Is this gravely to be called science? The fish's tail is its great organ of locomotion, and a marvellous one it is. Might we not suggest with more reason, that if there were any such development at all, it " might come to be worked in " as legs? But as the Darwinian system is founded upon similarities, the tail of the fish being at its nether end, the quadruped, the descendant of the fish, must have been similarly furnished!

As in the sea, so in certain lakes (perhaps in many others) there are shoals of gregarious fishes, caught like the herring or pilchard in nets stretched along the coasts.

There is the pollan of Lough Neagh, the agone of the Lake of Como, and a similar gregarious fish in the Lake of Geneva. It is difficult to conceive how these different fish, partaking of the same gregarious habits, but in other respects quite distinct, could have proceeded from a common progenitor, and taken up their separate abodes in these lakes, as it is difficult to imagine a communication between lakes so distant from one another. No doubt we shall be furnished with one or more conjectural explanations, dignified with the adjunct scientific, like these profound conjectures with respect to the tail of mammals.

That Darwinism supposes that cats exist because they catch mice well, and that it is the condition of their existence, seems a simple truism; in other words, that cats exist because they are provided with the means and power of obtaining their food, otherwise they could not live. "That cats exist *in order* to catch mice well" would certainly be a strange teleogical argument; unless it only means that they exist in order to keep down the excess of the very voracious rats, mice, and small birds, which, unchecked, would soon eat up a country.

Vegetation must have been first created to afford food for the innumerable herbivora of all kinds, as without it they could not have existed; and the carnivora, whether cats, wolves, tigers, or lions, again, to keep down the excess of the herbivora, perhaps also to save them from a lingering death by starvation and old age. The poisonous snake, again, may possibly have been destined to check the too great increase of the carnivora.

Sir Charles Lyell* quotes Mr. Wallace's argument on the long neck of the giraffe. "Changes," says Mr. Wallace, "have been brought about, not by the volition of the creatures themselves, but by the survival of varieties which had the greatest facilities of obtaining their food. The giraffe did not acquire its long neck by desiring to reach the foliage of lofty trees, and by constantly stretching out its neck for that purpose, but varieties which occurred with a longer neck than usual had an advantage over their shorter-necked companions, and on the first scarcity of food were enabled to survive them."

Now we have the duck with a short neck, the goose with a longer one, and the swan with the longest neck of the three, and all three have remained, as we know from ancient

* "Principles of Geology," vol. ii. p. 281.

representations, for thousands of years past with the same proportional length of neck. But the duck, turning up its little tail vertically, has struggled for these thousand years, and struggles still, to pick up its food from the bottom of ponds and rivers, as the giraffe has stretched out its neck " to reach the foliage of lofty trees," and the goose and the swan, like the duck, have been similarly employed. Why should not varieties of the longer neck, as well as the giraffe, have "had an advantage" over the shorter-necked duck, and all our geese have become swans? According to Mr. Wallace's argument, ducks and geese should have become long-necked birds like the swan. The giraffe, instead of being furnished with a long neck, through the extinction of the shorter-necked giraffes, of the existence of which we have not a particle of evidence, might just as well have acquired shorter, instead of their preposterous, fore-legs, in order to enable it to pick up its food from the ground; a larger field for food than the foliage of trees. At present, in order to pick up food from the ground, it is obliged to straddle out its forelegs with difficulty—an inconvenient process which would just as likely have been corrected in the struggle for existence by the shortening of the legs. There is scarcely an animal in existence some of the limbs of which might not be theoretically improved, according to these views of apparent expediency; but all such limbs, as far as we know hitherto, have been exactly contrived to fulfil, without change of any kind, the objects of the existence of the animals to which they belong. We have no knowledge of such "changes having been brought about."

It seems a mere shallow conjecture, dignified with the name of scientific. Professor Huxley and F. Müller allege that the opponents of their arguments must infer caprice in the work of the Creator. Messrs. Darwin and Wallace's arguments lead to the inference that the creations of the Almighty were defective, and not sufficiently adapted to the purposes for which they were created—that the shorter-necked mythical giraffe was in fact a blunder. Verily a new scientific system of jumping at conclusions. To instance another. Mr. Darwin* lays it down as a "corollary of the highest importance that the structure of every organic being is related in the most essential, yet hidden, manner to that of all other organic beings with which it comes into competition for food

---

* "Origin of Species," p. 77.

or residence, or from which it has to escape, or on which it preys. This is obvious in the structure of the teeth and talons of the tiger, and in that of the parasite which clings to the hair on the tiger's body." Here is a grand generalisation; but is it true? the wolf, bear, hyæna, jackal, come into "competition for food" with the feline races; but the one set has toes and nails, the others claws. So the horse has hoofs, the ox cloven feet. If the parasite of the tiger, "on which it preys," has legs and claws like his victim, are we to infer that the parasite of the horse has hoofs, of the ox cloven feet, or of man, our enemy the flea or louse, five fingers? One would be glad also to learn whereabouts in the long chain of beings "from one primordial form" in "the ordinary succession by generation," our parasite is to be placed, and what relationship the parasite of man bears to man.

How can the various species of deer be said to have a "structure related in the most essential manner" to the lion, panther, &c., from which they have to escape? Certainly not in the terminations of the feet. Darwin also refers to the destruction of organs through "natural selection." * He says:— "What can be plainer than that the webbed feet of ducks and geese are formed for swimming? yet there are upland geese with webbed feet which rarely or never get near the water, and no one except Audubon has seen the frigate bird, which has all its toes webbed, alight on the surface of the sea." He also says, "The deeply scooped membrane between the toes shows that structure has

* "Origin of Species," p. 185.

begun to change." It is difficult to believe that the frigate bird does not alight on the surface of the sea, either for washing, of which birds are fond, or for sleeping or repose, like any other sea-bird. Audubon is the only witness to prove the fact; but have other witnesses been examined, and of the thousands of sailors, how many would there be who would take any notice whatever of the fact? For aught we know, the frigate bird may take his rest on the sea at night, when it would be impossible, or difficult at all events, to see them. As for the upland goose, water or no water, web-footed like the frigate bird it still remains, and disuse of its web has not destroyed it. It is said that South Sea Island babies can swim almost before they can walk. They ought, according to the theory of the acquisition of organs by use, to have lost the power of walking, and their toes have become web-footed by natural selection. Perhaps we shall be told that they will become so in millions of years if they remain during those years in the same conditions of existence. But this is not likely. Physical, let alone moral, conditions and changes of the earth's surface, are, we are told, and no doubt truly, always going on; therefore the Otaheitan babies have a poor chance of getting time enough for the convenience of acquiring webbed feet, and this surely is the case with every other living creature on the face of the earth. We may *conjecture* that these changes of structure by natural selection might take place, but we may be very sure, or at all events have presumptive evidence, that they never will, as they never have, in the whole experience of man.

When we consider the infinite creations of the whole universe—the stars, or suns, and worlds of infinite variety, which our telescopes can disclose, with the conviction of the existence of an infinity of others which they cannot disclose; when we reflect upon the possibility, or rather probability of these worlds, infinite in number, containing living organisms in an infinity heaped upon infinity, that we should have any difficulty in imagining an infinite variety of separate creations of the organic beings upon earth, seems unreasonable, to say the least. To substitute for this a theory founded upon conjectures derived from a few isolated and doubtful facts respecting varieties, the theory of the progress in development of all organic beings from some one, or four, or five primordial forms, in the ordinary succession by generation, in the teeth of the fact that all genera and species too, as far as wild or semi-wild animals are concerned, abhor intermixture, seems still more unreasonable.*

Professor Tyndal, commenting upon the miracle at Gibeon, " Sun, stand thou still; and thou, Moon, on the valley of Ajalon," says, " The energy here involved is equal to that of trillions of horses working for the whole of the time employed by Joshua in the destruction of his foes." And again, " The same lavish squandering of energy stares the scientific man in the face. . . . . To other miracles similar remarks apply. Transferring thought from our little sand-grain of an earth to the immeasurable heavens, where

* For instance, the closely allied species, the red and fallow deer, will not breed together in their semi-domesticated condition in a park.

countless worlds, with their freights of life, probably revolve unseen; . . . . and bringing this face to face with the idea that the Builder and Sustainer of it all should contract Himself to a burning bush, or behave in other familiar ways ascribed to Him, it is easy to understand how astounding the incongruity must appear to the scientific man. Did this credulous prattle of the ancients about miracles stand alone; were it not locally associated with words of imperishable wisdom, and with examples of moral grandeur unmatched elsewhere in the history of the human race, both the miracles and their evidences would have long since ceased to be the transmitted inheritance of intelligent men. Under the pressure of the awe which this universe inspires, well may we exclaim in David's spirit, if not in his words—'When

I consider the heavens the work of Thy fingers, the moon and the stars which Thou hast ordained; what is man that Thou should be mindful of him, or the son of man that Thou shouldst so regard him.'"*

Naturally impressed with "the awe which this universe inspired," scientific men must be equally impressed, as were the scientific Kirby and Spence, with the fact "that of innumerable species of insects, many of them beyond conception fragile and exposed to dangers and enemies without end, no link should be lost from the chain, but all be maintained in those relative proportions necessary for the good of the system; that if one species for a while preponderates, and, instead of preserving, seems to destroy, yet counterchecks should at the same time be provided to reduce

---

* "Fragments of Science," p. 446.

it within its due limits; and further, that the operations of insects should be so directed as to effect the purposes for which they were created, and never exceed their commission."*

Not only therefore has the Creator established laws for the preservation of the harmony of the immeasurable universe above us, but has also condescended to establish similar laws for the myriads of the minutest of his creations in this "our little sand-grain of earth." Some of these purely physical laws we seem to have discovered, many others are utterly perplexing and beyond our ken. Still more perplexing are the moral laws which govern the intelligent world of his creation. Science cannot reach them. But we cannot believe that his care has not extended to his

* "Introduction to Entomology," Kirby and Spence, vol. i. p. 19.

intelligent creation mankind, as well as to his creations of inert matter and unintelligent organisms. Well indeed may we share in David's astonishment that the Infinite Being should be "mindful" of man, as well as of the greatest and minutest objects of his creation, from the impossibility of our finite ideas comprehending the infinite.

But it will be said that He has established laws for the human race which equally govern the existence of the intelligent as of the unintelligent creatures of the earth—physical laws for the former as for the latter. But there is something inherent in the nature of man which no other creatures possess—the intellectual faculties; for it is absurd to compare them with the instinct of animals; the glimmer of reason which Mr. Darwin endeavours to show in animals, compared with human intellectual faculties, is as the light of a candle to the noonday sun; it is but another similarity which man shares with animals in material form, but a similarity in which there is scarcely more than a faint likeness. Mankind requires something more than the physical laws which regulate his material existence; his intellectual existence requires the guidance of moral laws, without which the race would dwindle and perish from off the face of the earth. Man enjoys a freedom of action for good or evil. The moral laws are the restraint which controls the abuse of his powers, and some kind of religion has been found necessary by all nations in the whole history of the earth (even the monsters of the French Revolution discovered the necessity of establishing the worship of the "Être Suprême") in order to give strength and influence to the moral laws. If science may discover the instincts and physical laws which preserve all living creatures in the order and proportions in which they are so wonderfully preserved, science must also acknowledge the intellectual attributes for good or evil of man, and the moral laws which preserve the race of men in a similar, though by no means the same, order and proportions. Religion, without which moral laws are but fine words or waste paper,* and may be called a science, the object of which is to discover the purest form in which is taught the super-

---

* Moral laws, without the sanction and authority of religion, will only be observed as long as it is expedient to observe them. All the fine moral arguments in the world will not prevent certain men from lying if they be secure against detection. Alas, many other such infractions of the moral laws might be enumerated. One that has always struck me as unaccountable, is the horrible cruelty with which some slave-owners were wont to treat their unhappy slaves, for that was not even an expedient breach of the law.

intending authority and care of the Deity, who hates and will punish sin, and loves and will reward righteousness—the science which teaches of the Creator as other sciences teach of his creations, and therefore of the highest interest to thinking, intelligent men.

Apart, therefore, from any revelation, we may with sound reason believe, as I have said before, that the Creator would not leave his intelligent creatures without some knowledge of his Will; and that the communication of that Will has been transmitted in a certain manner, that is, through one nation, to mankind, as we have independent and ample evidence to prove. It is difficult indeed to imagine how otherwise it could have been transmitted; and how could we know that that heavenly Will did really come from heaven, except by the exercise of heavenly powers altogether beyond the powers of man, that is, by miracle? The Baptist in prison sends his disciples to ask of Christ, "Art thou he that should come, or do we look for another?" The answer was, "Go and show John again those things which ye do hear and see: the blind receive their sight and the lame walk; the lepers are cleansed, and the deaf hear; the dead are raised up, and the poor have the Gospel preached to them." Could any other answer be satisfactory to the prisoner, any other logical proof be given of the heavenly nature of the mission of Christ? It would be contrary to common sense for any one to say this mode of God's dealings with man was impossible; all he could say would be that it was improbable. He should then follow the example of the Baptist prisoner, and inquire into the evidence to accept or reject it at his own peril. Though we may cavil at a belief in miracles of which we only read, and be cautious of accepting them on account of the many false imitations, explain it as you will, we have the standing miracle of the Jewish dispersion, and of the persistent existence and strange characteristics of that other branch of the race, the sons of Ishmael, prophesied thousands of years ago (see Newton, " On the Prophesies "), always before our eyes, to afford us evidence not to be found in any other history of the extraordinary character, and a rational conviction, of the sacred truth of the Bible. We are not, therefore, left entirely to the evidence of history; not, however, that we have any reasonable ground for withholding our faith from that history. Incredulity is often as foolish as credulity. As " scientific men " have so often and recently declared things of science to be impossible, objectionable, or useless (see p. 275), which have turned out perfectly possible and of the greatest advantage, we need not be surprised at, or believe any of their assertions of the impossibility or the improbability of a real or apparent break in the continuity of the laws of creation at the fiat of the Creator. Such assertions may be considered the presumptuous incredulity of scientific men. Whether the sun and moon hastening not to go down for a whole day was a real or apparent phenomenon we cannot know, but to estimate the forces required at trillions, or twenty trillions of horse-power, and to assume that exercise of power to have been too great for the occasion, seems to be the assuming of a knowledge which is beyond our ken altogether. How can we estimate the importance of any event to the moral world, trifling as it may appear in our eyes, to the great scheme of law which must govern the world of intelligence, or count up the amount of dead material force which it would be worth while to exercise to bring about the event? To assign limits to the infinite almighty power of God, or to suppose that trillions of horse-power are great or small in his sight, would be but a low and unphilosophic view. As well might we say that it was not *tanti* to stop the 2,000 horse-power engines of an ironclad to prevent the running down of a child in a skiff.

Professor Tyndal does not indeed appear to hold so enlarged and philosophic a view of the Infinite Being, the Creator of the universe, as we find in both the Old and New Testament. As we see in Nature the same wonderful and, as I may say, careful adaptation of means to end in the smallest as in the largest object of creation, and the same order as in the whole universe of stars and planets, as far as our knowledge extends, so we see in the Bible the conception of infinite greatness and power and of a condescension to the lowest of his intelligent creations on the part of the Almighty Creator. There He is found as the Creator of heaven and earth, and yet He speaks with Adam and Eve. He speaks with Moses in the flaming fire in the bush, and before the people of Israel in the awful grandeur of the thunders of Mount Sinai. "But will God indeed dwell on the earth? Behold, the heaven, and heaven of heavens, cannot contain thee; how much less this house that I have builded!"* "For thus

* 1 Kings viii. 27.

saith the high and lofty One that inhabiteth eternity, whose name is Holy; I dwell in the high and holy place, with him also that is of a contrite and humble spirit to revive the spirit of the humble, and to revive the heart of the contrite ones;"* and again he speaks with Elijah—"And, behold, the Lord passed by, and a great and strong wind rent the mountains, and brake in pieces the rocks before the Lord; but the Lord was not in the wind: and after the wind an earthquake; but the Lord was not in the earthquake: and after the earthquake a fire; but the Lord was not in the fire: and after the fire a still small voice."† "Whither shall I go then from thy Spirit, or whither shall I go then from thy presence? If I climb up to heaven Thou art there. If I go down to hell Thou

* Isaiah lvii. 15. † 1 Kings xix. 11, &c.

art there also."* In the New Testament—"Are not five sparrows sold for two farthings, and not one of them is forgotten before God?"† Many other passages might be cited to show how lofty, indeed how philosophical a conception of the Creator, with whom there can be neither great or small, beginning or end, is the conception of Jew and Christian derived from the Bible. The "incongruity" so astounding to some scientific men, can be no incongruity to others who have not so low a conception of the Creator of the universe. If, however, the Professor is still astounded, he may perhaps be more reconciled to the passage as interpreted by St. Stephen before his martyrdom; for he says, there appeared to Moses "in the wilderness of Mount Sinai an *angel of the Lord* in a flame of fire in the bush."‡

---

* Psalm cxxxix. 6, 7.   † Luke xii. 6.   ‡ Acts vii. 30.

And again, in a subsequent verse, "The same (*i.e.* Moses) did God send to be a ruler and a deliverer by the *hand of the angel* which appeared to him in the bush." The Professor is hard upon our ancestors for their belief in and punishment of witches and wizards, but surely the séance at which he was present shows that there are people in England, as there are also in America and elsewhere, who believe in an intercourse with spirits, the very same belief as that which constituted the witch. Even table-turning, by some of the adepts employed for purposes of witchcraft, is shown to be only a repetition of an ancient form of witchcraft by A. de Broglie, who gives his ancient authorities : " Trois officiers, nommés Pergannus, Fédusius et Irénée, aidés de deux magiciens Patricius et Hilaire, avaient conçu . . . le désir de connoître quel serait le successeur de Valens. Pour satisfaire leur curiosité ils avaient eu recours à une pratique de sorcellerie fort en usage à cette époque, et qui consistait . . . à mettre en mouvement sans aucune impulsion extérieure, et uniquement par des rites magiques, une petite table de laurier reposant sur trois pieds. La table portait un disque de metal sur la face duquel étaient gravées les 24 lettres de l'alphabet. Quand on avait réussi à la faire entrer dans un mouvement de rotation sur elle-même, on approchait un anneau suspendu à un fil qui, frappant dans ses oscillations tantôt une lettre tantôt une autre, arrivait à former des syllabes, puis des mots ; . . . enfin . . . ils avaient vu distinctement l'anneau et la table former par leur rencontre les deux syllabes Théod."* Here we have

* "L'Eglise et l'Empire Romain," vol. v. p. 308.

table-turning in the fourth century, with the trifling modification of the alphabet and ring; but perhaps these may be used by some modern necromancers.

In the results of these and similar magical pretensions, which evil results sometimes show themselves in the form of insanity, and sometimes in the form of swindling a friend, we may see a good reason for prohibiting, *i.e.* punishing them, let alone the blasphemous nonsense which is sometimes their fruit. Even now we punish the poor wise woman who tells fortunes with cards or other devices. The belief in the existence of spirits, good or bad, is, however, not without a very reasonable ground; for we cannot believe, indeed one may say it is a stupid presumption to assume, that our intelligence is the highest in creation, or that intelligence must be inseparably connected with substance such as ours. Scientific men, from Newton to Faraday, have had a very strong faith in the Christian religion, which obliges a belief in the Bible, in miracles, and this belief in spirits. The unscientific may set the opinions of the great genius of science, Professor Faraday, against those of Professor Tyndal. Swedenborg, one of the first scientific men of his day, respected by philosophers as well as potentates, not only believed in the existence of spirits, but asserted that he conversed with them, and the evidence of his having had such communication with them was satisfactory to Baron Grimm, Professor Schlegel, and Immanuel Kant. It is clearly, therefore, unwise to put implicit faith in the opinions of "scientific men," except in matters relating to their own special science, and not always even then, especially if they be French; according to Professor Huxley, not in any case until you have the "absolute authority of Nature." The belief in the existence of spirits has been the rational belief of the wisest of men of all time, and generally of all men; no wonder, therefore, that men should have a yearning desire to penetrate the mystery. But it is one thing to believe in the existence of spirits, and that they may be made apparent to our senses under extraordinary circumstances — quite another thing to believe that we can call them at our will "from the vasty deep" by the help of male or female mediums or the legs of wooden tables. Imposture is for the most part an imitation of truth, and so far we are indebted to Professor Tyndal for exposing an instance of delusion if not imposture.

Professor Huxley's "Lay Sermon on Darwinism" would lead the reader to imagine that science would be a wholesome substitute for religion, and Sir J. Lubbock, inferentially, contrasts unfavourably the teaching of religion with the teachings of science. The latter writes, "Men do wrong, either from ignorance, or in the unexpressed hope that they may enjoy the pleasure and yet avoid the penalty of sin. In this respect there can be no doubt that religious teaching is widely mistaken. Repentance is too often regarded as a substitute for punishment."* Is it not certain that men do often enjoy the pleasure and avoid the penalty of sin in this world? Alas, we all know too well that there are such people as prosperous profligates of all kinds, and unless they have the conscience which religion

* "Pre-historic Times," p. 489.

teaches to alarm them, their pleasure is unalloyed by penalty of any kind. Sir J. Lubbock appears to have but a slight acquaintance with "religious teaching" of the meaning of repentance. Religion does not teach that repentance is a "substitute for punishment." Repentance is required for sin, whether followed by punishment or not. It is not regret alone for sin committed, but includes a determination not to sin again, independently of all idea of the results of sin.

The following explanation of Lactantius, to whom the language of Scripture was a living language, and to whom the translation of the Greek word for repentance in the New Testament could then be no difficulty, may be of use to those who have mistaken the "teaching of religion" with respect to repentance; but, if Protestants, they must be the very ignorant indeed.

"Is enim qui facti sui pœnitet, errorem suum pristinum intelligit: idioque Græci melius et significantius μετάνοιαν dicunt; quem nos possumus resipiscentiam dicere; resipiscit enim ac mentam suam quasi at insaniâ recipit, quem errati piget, castigatque seipsum dementiæ, et confirmat animum suum ad rectius vivendum; tum illud ipsum maxime cavet, ne rursus in eosdem laqueos indicatur. Denique muta animalia cum fraude capiuntur si aliquo se modo in fugam extricaverint, sunt postmodum cautiora; vitantque semper se omnia, in quibus dolos insidiasque senserunt. Sic hominem pœnitentiâ cautum, se diligentum facit ad evitanda peccata, in quæ semel fraude deciderit. Et idcirco Deus imbecillitatem nostram sciens, pro sue pietate aperuit hominis portum salutis; ut huic necessitate cui fragilitas nostra subjecta est medicina pœnitentiæ subveniret."*

"For he who repents of his action, understands his former error; so the Greeks use the word μετάνοιαν (change of mind) better and with more significance, which we may call, 'resipiscentiam' (a coming to one's senses again); for he comes to his senses, and recovers his mind from a state of insanity, who grieves at his error, and chastises himself for his madness, and fortifies his mind for living a better life; besides that, his greatest care is lest he should be led into the like snares. Indeed, even dumb animals also, when they are taken by snares, if in any way they can extricate themselves, become afterwards more cautious, and avoid always

* Lactantius, lib. vi. 24.

those things in which they perceive guile or snares. Thus repentance makes man cautious and careful to avoid those sins in which he once had fallen through guile. For no one can be so prudent, so circumspect, as that he should not sometimes fall. And therefore God, knowing our weakness, has in his pity opened a harbour of safety to men, that the medicine of repentance should come to the relief of this need to which our frailty is subject."

The same interpretation of repentance is to be found in both the Old and New Testament, where we seek our religious teaching. Solomon, at the dedication of the Temple, says, "Yet if they shall bethink themselves in the land whither they are carried captives, and repent, and make supplication unto Thee; . . . . . and so *return unto Thee* with all their heart and soul," &c.* In St. Matthew, "*Bring forth therefore fruits* meet for repentance."†

St. Paul also says, he "showed first unto them of Damascus, &c., that they should repent and turn to God, and do *works meet for repentance.*"

All these teachings, as well as the whole tenor of Scripture, plainly show that repentance is not a "substitute for punishment;" and if it implies sorrow for past sins, it also implies a determination not to return to them.

Sir John Lubbock goes the length of saying, "that the great principle of natural selection is to biology what the law of gravitation is to astronomy." This is indeed comparing great things with small. To compare the discovery of the great law which

* 1 Kings viii. 47, 48. † Matt. iii. 8.

governs all bodies in the heavens and the earth with that of natural selection, or the survival of the fittest, which, shorn of its scientific pretensions, resolves itself into the obvious rule that the stronger and healthier animals will get the better of and survive the weaker animals of any species, for the conservation of the race, is a remarkable feature in modern scientific thought, and might be considered the discovery of a mare's nest as compared with the great discovery of Newton.

A philosophical deism tends to produce a virtual atheism. The great mass of mankind see the most elaborate contrivance of the ingenuity of man without a thought of the contriver; in fact, in a few generations his name almost passes away. Is it not the same with the marvellous works of God? Who but the very thoughtful, as well as intellectual, ever connect any of those works with the idea of Him who created them? A substantive and formulated creed is surely necessary for the welfare of mankind in general, and a sense of Eternal over-ruling justice as a deterrent from crime and of Eternal mercy as an encouragement to virtue, in order to control the evil passions, and the abuse of the innocent passions, inherent in our natures.

Scientific research opens our eyes to the fact that the Creator has bestowed the same care on the minutest as on the greatest of his unintelligent creations of the physical world. We cannot therefore, with Sir C. Bell, believe that his care has not extended to the intelligent creations of the moral world, or that He has left the moral world "in all that disarray which our partial view would persuade us they are." We have therefore a scientific reason for believing that He has extended his care to the moral world, in the communication of his Will to his intelligent creatures. This has been the rational belief of some of the wisest and the scientific of mankind for ages; and in the words of an address of Mr. Harper's—"It must be remembered that these writings (the Bible) were in the first place intended for a semi-barbarous race recently rescued from the debasing influences of slavery, and afterwards for all people and all classes of all time, of whom the savans form an inappreciably minute number. It is not one of the least extraordinary attributes of the Bible, that a book of such unparalleled antiquity should have escaped the many destructions with which it has been threatened, and preserved for so many ages an unexampled respect," &c. Mr. Harper might have added that the Jews alone of all the surrounding nations who had a literature, Phœnicians, &c., preserved these their writings. With their literature those other nations have utterly perished, as foretold by the prophets, and as by them foretold in these very writings the Jews alone survive, scattered over the face of the earth. It is also not a little remarkable that the literature of the Greeks and Romans, so essential to our understanding of the New Testament, has been providentially preserved amidst the general wreck of the literature of other nations. "The unexampled respect" for the Bible some scientific men are endeavouring to destroy. Two generations have now had experience of the results of that destruction in France and elsewhere, where the blood-thirsty monsters who had lost that respect proclaimed murder, arson, robbery, and violence of all sorts as their miserable creed, or rather want of creed. Voltaire, infidel as he was, had the sense to see, and to warn men in some of his writings, of the danger which, however, he had not the sense to see he was doing his utmost to create by his other works. In his " Homélie sur l'Athéisme," he says:*—"Si le monde était gouverné par des athées, il vaudrait autant être sous l'empire de ces êtres infernaux qu'on nous peint acharnés contre leurs victimes." And in his letter to Villeviellet†—"Je veux que les princes et les ministres reconnaissent un Dieu, et même un Dieu qui punisse et pardonne. Sans ce frein, je les regarderai comme des animaux féroces, . . . mais que certainement me mangeront s'ils me rencontrent sous leurs griffes quand ils auront faim," &c.

* Vol. xxxii. p. 147. † Vol. ix. p. 523.

The past history of France has proved Voltaire's shrewdness in seeing the evil, and folly in not seeing how much he was doing to promote it. Some of our scientific men are following in his footsteps, less directly, but perhaps more insidiously. If not therefore indifferent to the welfare of mankind—perhaps of their own kith and kin—they should not make use of crude theories, doubtful inferences from often contradictory evidence, and scientific, or so-called scientific facts, to undermine the authority of the Bible, and, with it, Christianity. If they persist, careless of the lessons of the past, instead of being our material benefactors, as so many have been, they will be the execration of generations to come, should history, as it is too probable, repeat itself.

It is curiously and instructively interesting

to read in the life of Voltaire, prefixed to the edition of his works of 1789—"Si l'amour de l'humanité est devenue le langage commun de tous les hommes; si les guerres sont devenues moins fréquentes; . . . si pour la première fois la raison commence à répandre sur tous les peuples de l'Europe un jour égal et pur; partout dans l'histoire de ces changemens on trouvera le nom de Voltaire."

If Condorcet could have read the future, he would have been compelled to acknowledge the utter falsehood of this eulogium. The "amour de l'humanité" was the general condemnation and persecution to death in general of all who differed in opinion from the party in power; instead of the "guerres moins fréquentes," wars of almost unparalleled magnitude and frequency; and as to the reason "égal et pur," as they were so they continued to be, pretty words without meaning. In fact, France was, soon after the date when those words were written, writhing as it were in the tortures of delirium, her children decimated, and the seeds of misfortune sown to grow up for a harvest of misery about every twenty years until now.

The horrible tortures and executions for offences and imaginary offences against the superstitious tyranny of the Roman Church were enough to rouse the indignation of such a man as Voltaire, and, like so many Frenchmen, to make him fall from one extreme to another, and this opposite extreme seems to produce the same bitter fruits of cruelty and tyranny, as we have so recently seen in the diabolical and senseless murders and arson committed by the monsters of the Commune of Paris. Scientific men may destroy in the minds of many, as bad and ignorant men have debased or perverted, the Christian religion—the purest and most authentic ever known to man; but scientific men and philosophers never have built up, and never can be expected to build up, a moral edifice with any amount of scientific material. Of all sciences it would be supposed that medical science, so intimately connected as it is with our physical, and, collaterally, with our moral well-being, ought to command the belief of civilised man; but how little influence has it on the conduct of men in general! Ignorance in many a case cannot be pleaded; indeed, Professor Huxley's "absolute authority of Nature," discovered by personal experience, has often no effect whatever. The international conspiracy against all property is one of the ugly fruits of the absence of all religion—

a miserable envy of the better condition of one's neighbour, or, in other words, a repudiation of the tenth Commandment, "Thou shalt not covet."

The deep-sea soundings, superintended by Dr. Carpenter, afford us evidence to prove that the deductions and ratiocinations of some scientific men are sometimes altogether erroneous. He says* that the soundings have shown "the existence of a varied and abundant submarine fauna at depths which have been generally supposed to be either altogether azoic or tenanted only by animals of a very low type," and that not even the total privation of light, which the highest authorities have affirmed to be essential to the existence of life, prevents these rayless

* "Lecture at the Royal Institution."—("Proceedings of the Royal Institution, &c.," vol. v. part vi. p. 506.)

depths of ocean from supporting a vast and continuous mass of life.* At p. 508 he shows how geologists "might easily fall into the mistake of supposing two such different faunæ occurring at different levels must indicate two distinct climates separated in time, instead of indicating, as they have been shown to do, two contemporaneous but dissimilar climates, separated only by a few miles horizontally and by 300 fathoms vertically."

Not many years ago a formidable array of scientific men, especially in France, endeavoured to prove the great antiquity of man, from the supposed and confidently asserted immense antiquity of the zodiacs of Dendera and Esneh, but their elaborate arguments came to a miserable conclusion after about twenty years' discussion, by the discovery that

* "Proceedings of the Royal Institution," vol. v. pt. vi. p. 504.

these monuments were of recent Roman imperial date. Some writers have endeavoured to produce other arguments for the antiquity of man, from the mythical histories of Egypt, India, and China, which, if they prove anything, prove the vanity and lying spirit of some of our race.

It will therefore be prudent to withhold our belief in the Darwinian theory and the immense antiquity of pre-historic man until we find better evidence for it than has hitherto been produced, lest the theory should share the fate of the deductions from the zodiacs of Dendera and Esneh.

THE DELUGE.

IN their monuments, histories, or records, the ancient nations of the Old World have left the tradition of a great deluge, involving the destruction of the human race, with the exception of a family or a few individuals. This tradition was preserved even by nations of the New World, and also in that newer world, Australia. Mr. E. B. Kennedy,* quoting James Morrill's account of the blacks, with whom he passed a miserable captivity of seventeen years, says, "They say their forefathers witnessed a great flood, and nearly all were drowned, only those who got on a very high mountan were saved." This

* "Four Years in Queensland," p. 84.

tradition, therefore, may be called an all but universal tradition among the nations of the earth, or, to use the words of Professor Hitchcock, a "scientific man" and a geologist, "It is well known that in the written and unwritten traditions of almost every tribe and nation under heaven, the story of a general deluge has been prominent."* All these traditions agree in referring the great catastrophe to a deluge. Attempts have been made to account for them by the suggestion that great floods have been common in most countries, and therefore it is not extraordinary that every nation should have attributed the great disaster to such a cause.

Why should all nations have agreed in handing down such a tradition at all if such an awful event never took place?

* "Religion of Geology," p. 104.

If it was a tradition handed down to posterity by the survivors of the nation that suffered, why should such a catastrophe have been almost universally described as affecting one family or two individuals? So overwhelming a flood is not common in the experience of mankind.

Again, why should all nations have unanimously attributed the destruction to a deluge?

Far more terrible local disturbances are of common occurrence in many countries. The earthquake for instance, so awfully sudden, so fearfully destructive, swallowing up whole towns, whole populations, and unlike other great natural agents of destruction, leaving an unconquerable feeling of terror. In many countries this would have been as likely to be assigned as the cause of the great catastrophe as a flood. This, or the volcano, might just as well have been supposed the destroying agent, especially in Mexico and Peru, not to mention many a country of the Old World.

Not only do all of these traditions agree in the main fact, but many of them agree also in some details. The ark, dove, or other bird, are to be found, curiously enough, in their emblematic representations of the deluge, so that Mexicans, pagan Greeks, and the Christians of the Catacombs, peoples so distant in time and place, have adopted a very similar mode of representing it. Figures of the Apamean medal, and the Christian representation of the ark from the cemetery of Callixtus at Rome, are given by Dr. Wiseman at p. 321 of his "Lectures," and Lord Kingsborough's great work, "The Mexican Representation." Thus the traditions of mankind are even in some details in strict accordance with the narrative of the Deluge contained in the Bible.

The author of that narrative has recorded the prophetic announcement of another very different, but perhaps more painful, catastrophe, the dispersion and degradation of the race to which he belonged. We see it now fulfilled to the letter, and neither time nor persecutions unnumbered have prevented the Jewish race from bearing witness to its fulfilment; but they, as well as too many others, have eyes that will not see, ears that will not hear, and understanding but they will not understand.

Without assuming any authority for the Pentateuch as the work of inspiration, and considering it only as a secular history of an event the remembrance of which has been preserved by the nations of the earth, let us consider whether the facts of geology, imperfect as is our knowledge of it, and the conjectures founded on that imperfection, are really, as some pretend, incompatible with this Biblical and universal tradition of the Deluge. It must always be borne in mind, that the few brief sentences in which the Deluge is described in Genesis are written in a dead and very ancient language, and therefore, that our translation may not give a perfect reflection of the original, word for word. That whatever there is in the history in the nature of detail, is given in the most general terms, and that it was written for the comprehension, not of scientific men, but primarily for a race of semi-barbarous and ignorant men, just emancipated from a cruel bondage, and in after-ages, as we have good reason to believe, for the great mass of the world of human beings. May we not fairly assume that words, to which in our translation we give an extended signification, ought to bear a limited one? For instance, the word we translate "earth" in the account of the Deluge, bears the signification of land, country, or region in other parts of the Pentateuch. "And the famine was over all the face of the earth." "And all countries came into Egypt to Joseph to buy corn."* "And there was no bread on the whole earth,"† according to Dr. Kalisch's translation. We must in reason infer that our translation of these passages has not caught the exact meaning of the original, and that the words "all," "the whole," and "the earth," ought

* Gen. xli. 56, 57.   † Ibid. xlvii. 13.

to bear a limited and not a universal meaning. Our version of Gen. xlvii. 13 is, "and there was no bread in *all the land*," whence it would appear that the words "on the *whole earth*" of Dr. Kalisch, and "in *all the land*" of our version, were in the Hebrew of doubtful signification, or admitting of either translation. That of our version seems, from the contrast, the more rational one. Dr. Kalisch, however, will not admit of any limitation in the case of the general expressions relating to the Deluge, but in his note to Exod. xxi. 6, where the words "for ever" are used, he quotes Rashbam to show that these words must, as they clearly must, be understood to mean "all the days of his life," and Ebn Ezra, who says that "for ever means a long time." Without the help of Rashbam or Ebn Ezra, we may fairly assume that, like the words "for ever," the other words referred to may, as in some instances they clearly must, bear a limited and not a universal meaning. But the substantive "earth," even in French or Italian, if dead languages, would admit of different interpretations. It would scarcely be a figurative expression to write "Toute la terre était couverte de neige," where the writer merely referred to the country around him. Yet the word "terre," if French were a dead language, might be translated either the *earth* or the *land*.

But it is not only in the Old Testament that we find words having a limited signification to which we apply a general or universal one in our translation, for we find them also in the New Testament. "And there were dwelling at Jerusalem devout men out of every nation under heaven;"* "And how hear we every man in our own tongue wherein we were born?"† and then enumerating the nations, and therefore limiting the expression "under the whole heaven." Again,‡ "the truth of the Gospel which is come unto you as it is in all the world;" and in verse 23, "the hope of the Gospel which was preached to every creature under heaven." In fact, it would be easy to show that, even in modern languages, a translation may be literally correct, although idiomatically wrong. Another instance we find in St. Luke, chap. ii. verse 1, "There went out a decree from Cesar Augustus that all the world ($\pi\alpha\sigma\alpha\nu$ $\tau\eta\nu$ $o\iota\chi o\upsilon\mu\acute{e}\nu\eta\nu$) should be taxed," implying of course those parts of the world under the rule of Cesar. After the Deluge, we find (Gen., chap. viii.

* Acts ii. 5.   † Ibid. ii. 8.   ‡ Col. i. 5, 6.

verse 21), "I will not curse the *ground* any more for man's sake." Why should not the rendering here have been the *earth*, as in other passages of a similar import? We may therefore assume that these words, if the same in the Hebrew, may be used interchangeably as "earth," "country," "ground," or "region." It can hardly be supposed that Moses, whether writing under the influence of his own inspired authority, or quoting the writings of others on which he set his imprimatur, or writing without that inspiration which enabled him to foresee and foretell the fate of the Jewish people, was ignorant of the vast quantity of animals and reptiles of Africa, and that if he had meant that literally all the animals of the whole globe were brought into the ark, he would not have made some allusion to the extraordinary manner in which they were so brought from all parts of the earth. At the same time it must be considered that as we find the remains of the elk and the reindeer in the caves of Lebanon (see p. 270), and those of a variety of other animals now confined to limited spaces in tropical, and no longer in temperate zones, a far greater number of species may have been in existence before and in the region of the Deluge than at the present day. Where it is said, "I will cause it to *rain* upon the earth forty days and forty nights," we may safely suppose that the rain which fell on one part of the earth may have fallen in the shape of snow, though not specially mentioned, in another part at a higher altitude or in less temperate zones, nor can it be called a forced interpretation. "Fifteen cubits upward did the waters prevail; and the mountains were covered."* After the rain had fallen a hundred and fifty days, it began to abate, and continued to abate from before the seventeenth day of the seventh month, when the ark stranded, until the tenth month (*i.e.* nearly three months), when on the first day of the tenth month, the tops of the mountains were seen. As it is impossible to see any distance through heavy rain or driving sleet and snow, the tops of the mountains covered with snow may have been the mountains seen when the great fall had ceased, which till then could not have been seen. This view is in some measure confirmed by the absence of the raven, which Noah at first sent forth at the end of forty days from the first of the tenth month, and the return of the dove, for the raven could find a rest for the soles of its

* Gen. vii. 20.

feet on the snow, and food in the body of some dead animal, but the snow would have been no resting-place for the delicate dove, and food there would have been none for her.

Any one describing a great exceptional fall of rain over the whole of the British Isles, would not think it necessary to specify that the rain fell in the shape of snow on our mountains. We do not expect in rainfall tables any mention of the depth of snow which may have fallen on the mountains of Scotland or elsewhere. We could not, therefore, expect to find in the very concise description in Genesis of the Deluge, any mention of snow, and unless we found there a special assertion that rain and rain only fell, it is a fair presumption that in higher latitudes, or on lofty mountains, snow may have taken the place of rain, in the usual course of Nature's operations.

Mr. Stopford Brooke, in one of his sermons, tells us "the Hebrew language has more than ten different words for different kinds of rain." It would not be therefore surprising to find that we had not discovered the exact meaning of one of these ten words in so ancient a book as the Pentateuch.

Geology teaches us that at a certain period of the earth's history intense cold prevailed in temperate and even tropical latitudes. Many a valley in every country belonging to the present and last configuration of the earth's crust bears witness to the effects of glacial action, combined perhaps with great floods from the melting of the snow and ice which once covered the land. Rocks were ground by the ice into gravel or sand, and the sides of valleys heaped up with vast confused masses of stones, sand, and débris; and the groovings and striæ on rocky surfaces, the moutonnés or polished rocks, the transported blocks, such as we now see caused by ice and snow and modern glaciers, attest the former existence of what are called glacial periods. Some of the transported blocks of stone, carried to a great distance, deposited by floating icebergs, belonging to another period, when the present earth's surface was submerged; but others, belonging to our period, may have been transported, not by icebergs, but by the "calotte" of snow which covered the mountains. For the blocks seen on icebergs at sea must once have been in or on the ice before it broke away from the glacier, and might have been deposited on terra-firma by the melting of the ice or snow before it could reach the sea. That the calotte, or great mantle of ice or snow on lofty mountains, is a moving body (viscous or plastic) there is little doubt; consequently, any mass of rock detached from its parent mountain, and falling on its surface would be carried to a distance on the surface of the moving calotte. If I recollect rightly one of the difficulties attending the plan for a northern telegraphic communication with America, *via* Iceland and Greenland, was said to be the impossibility of carrying the wires on posts across the snows of Greenland in consequence of this motion. Dr. Kane shows,* not theoretically but by actual observation, the manner in which these transported blocks and rocking-stones are deposited, not under water, but on dry land by the snow. He says, "the rocks which

* "Arctic Explorations," vol. ii. p. 227.

fall in this manner (from the cliffs) upon the ice-belt were rapidly imbedded by the action of the sun's heat; and it happened frequently, of course, that one more recently disengaged would overlie another that had actually sunk below the surface. This, as the ice-belt subsided in the gradual thaw, had given many examples of the rocking-stone. I have placed in the margin some drawings of these geological puzzles. They were of all sizes, from tons to pounds, often strangely dissimilar in material, though grouped within a narrow area, their diversity depending on the varying strata from which they came."

Professor Charles Martens[*] has shown that the evidences of a glacial period are to be found in many places in both hemispheres. Agassiz found traces of glaciers in the Brazils.

[*] "Revue des Deux Mondes," 1867.

Sir W. Denison, in a letter to Sir R. Murchison,* (the answer unfortunately is not given), gives an account of many transported blocks or boulders near Kurnool, with sketches of two of them, one a very remarkable monument of the workings of Nature, a stone full 20 ft. in height standing upon two other stones about 10 ft. long. "The hills," he says, "on which are these stones, are bare of soil; in fact they rise out of the dry plain, looking as if they had been washed clean of all earth. A force capable of denuding the hills would, one would think, have destroyed the equilibrium of these balanced boulders." The above-cited observations of Dr. Kane appear amply sufficient to account for the curious position of these stones, and the melting of the snow and heavy rains for the denudation of the

* "Varieties of Viceregal Life," vol. ii. p. 278.

hills. It can hardly be supposed that icebergs deposited these blocks so nicely on the submerged hills, or that the subsequent action of the waves as the hills rose from the waters, would have left undisturbed the lofty stone on its narrow supports. It appears more probable that these stones were borne along by the calotte of snow, and deposited in the manner they are now in the arctic regions on its melting. In any case we have good reason to conclude that there was at some time or other a period of intense cold in tropical Hindostan as well as in the Brazils and Europe. We have yet to learn whether there is any evidence of a glacial period in Africa.

Whether this intense cold, this glacial period, prevailed over the whole earth at the same time or at different times no one can pretend to assert, but it would seem that if a glacial period prevailed in the tropics, it would probably extend to more temperate latitudes with a greater intensity, still greater again in the higher latitudes.* It will, however, be sufficient for our purpose to suppose that such a glacial period was that which caused the destruction of the human race by a deluge, wherever that race happened at the time to be existing. A glacial period, general, and taking place in the temperate zones of the earth, would be likely to produce great floods either at its commencement or as its intensity was moderating. We cannot

* Professor Forbes ("Norway and its Glaciers," p. 242) thinks it highly probable "that Norway was once nearly covered by ice and snow;" and at p. 243, "It is exceedingly probable that a diminution of the temperature of the summer months by 4° would at once place one-fourth of the surface of Norway within the snow-line."

give a precise meaning to the figurative expression, "the fountains of the great deep were broken up, and the windows (or floodgates) of heaven were opened." It is sufficient to understand by these, a great fall of rain, which in the higher latitudes and regions of the earth may have been snow, with perhaps great inroads of the sea, such as are often the effect of earthquakes, destroying all living things, together with man, in that part of the earth which they inhabited. Supposing, as before suggested, "the whole earth" of our translation changed to "the whole *country*," or region, and to imply that part of the earth inhabited by man, it would not follow that the destruction was so complete in other parts of the earth, where modified intensities of cold may have prevailed, and where mankind may not have penetrated, but where animals of some kinds may have escaped the great catastrophe. Considering how slow has been the growth of population in the historic period of Western Europe, we have more reason to suppose that mankind was at a far earlier period confined to a limited area of the earth's surface, than that the race should have spread over the whole earth. As a rule, all nations which retained any tradition of an origin, held that they were peoples who had migrated from elsewhere, driving out scanty populations, leaving no tradition, as the North American Indians are now, with all our advanced civilisation, being gradually exterminated or driven back into the wilderness.

As we find evidence of a high temperature having prevailed even in arctic regions at some period or periods in geological history, it is possible, or rather probable, that the hippopotamus, rhinoceros, elephant, and other now tropical animals, the remains of which have been found in Britain, France, Germany, Russia, and other now temperate latitudes, may have enjoyed before the Deluge a far better climate than we have now, and were able to exist where they could not at present; and although the Siberian elephant was clothed with a more hairy and woolly clothing than the Asiatic elephant, which however is provided with hair, it can scarcely be supposed that, even with such scanty clothing, the elephant could resist the severity of a Siberian winter.* It has been said that great heat would be required to produce a sub-

* The conjecture that the hippopotamus and other tropical animals may have made summer migrations from tropical to temperate latitudes can scarcely be accepted; a short swim would enable the hippopotamus to cross the Red Sea into Arabia, but such, I apprehend, is not his practice.

sequent great fall of rain and snow. If, therefore, the heat of the earth suited to the existence of those animals had been great before the Deluge, the evaporation, its consequence, would supply the excess of rain and snow, as the three years of unusual heat preceding the years 1770-71 have been succeeded by a severe winter and heavy floods. But I do not suppose scientific men are prepared to lay down the dictum, that the quantity of vapour in the atmosphere is a constant invariable quantity, incapable of increase or decrease by exceptional causes, astronomical or terrestrial, of which we are ignorant.

The tropical animals whose remains are found in so many parts of Europe may have been then destroyed by the excessive cold; and this, indeed, seems a rational way of accounting for the destruction of the vast herds of Siberian mammoths and the rhinoceros, coexistent maybe in time, but not necessarily in place, with antediluvian man, as well as other tropical animals, such as the hippopotamus, whose bones are found in Europe; some of these would then have been frozen up, and may have supplied man and animals with food many years after the Deluge, and before the intensity of the cold had disappeared in Western Europe, as the Siberian mammoth, &c., are now doing in Siberia. Other animals may have been swept away, mixed up with the bones of animals of aquatic habits; "tons of fractured bones of hippopotami"* may then have been huddled together in caverns and crevices of the rocks, as in Sicily. The rain, the snow, and the cold

* "Siluria," p. 492.

of the glacial period may not have prevailed to the same amount or with the same intensity over every part of the earth's surface, but specially over that portion of the world tenanted by man; many animals therefore, even non-migratory, may have survived the great cataclysm in other parts of the world, as many even now are able to resist the severity of an arctic winter, or as the tiger that of a Siberian climate.

Or we may suppose that the glacial period was not simultaneous in its effects over the whole earth, so that many animals may have survived, though locally destroyed altogether in that part of the earth which they shared with man. If by some great convulsion the Gulf-stream were diverted from its present course, either northwards, through Baffin's Bay into the arctic seas, or westward, either through a submergence of the Isthmus of Panama into the Pacific, or in some other direction, the climate of Europe, depending so much on the genial influence of the Gulfstream, would suffer a grievous reduction in temperature, and that genial influence would be transferred to other regions of the globe. The late Russian expedition has shown how powerful is that influence, preventing, as it appears, ice from forming even in the polar basin. The increase of temperature after the Flood, or glacial period, would probably have been gradual, and we find that Mount Lebanon had its glaciers before the historic period. "If," says Mr. H. B. Tristram, in his "Land of Israel," p. 11, "as Mr. Dawkins considers, these teeth are referable to those now exclusive quadrupeds, we have evidence of the reindeer and elk having been the food of man in the Lebanon not long before the historic period; for there is no necessity to put back to any date of immeasurable antiquity the deposition of these remains in a limestone cavern." This may be true; at the same time we must not forget that the bodies or remains of these animals may have been frozen up and been the food of man, as the animals of some remotely ancient glacial period are now eaten in Siberia. On the other hand, the elk and the reindeer may have existed before the Deluge in some of the intensely cold regions of Armenia, and have been preserved among the animals brought into the ark.

Without having recourse to the miraculous, or to that which appears to us a break in the order of Nature, there is no reason for assuming that Noah may not have brought together specimens of all the animals of the country over which the Deluge was to pass, as we have done in England and France in the Zoological Gardens or in the Jardin des Plantes, with animals from all parts of the earth, assigning, as before suggested, a limited interpretation to the words which in our translation bear a universal meaning, and supposing the animals brought into the ark to be those then existing in the region inhabited by men, and which was overwhelmed by the Great Flood, and not the animals existing in every part of the world. It seems reasonable to suppose that if all animals were destroyed in any great region by a flood, it would be necessary to provide a stock to take their place at its cessation, or the surviving men could not have existed after its subsidence, as the Prussians in the late war provided rations and the English provisions, to meet the wants of the Parisians when Paris ceased to be their ark. It may be objected that unclean animals and creeping things were also preserved, but we cannot pretend to know whether or not such creatures are necessary in the economy of Nature; indeed, the fact of their existence seems sufficient to entitle us to the belief that they are necessary.

Various may be the conjectures to explain the subsidence of so great a flood. Evaporation, some great subsidence where now is the Caspian Sea, or the earth opening her mouth on a great scale, as she has done in a small one in the island of Cephalonia, where the sea has been pouring into the earth in a continuous stream for years. If this wholly inexplicable phenomenon (for Professor Ansted's capillary theory can hardly be considered a satisfactory explanation)* were unknown, the impossibility of such an apparent exception to the law, that water finds its own level, would have been loudly declared. For aught we know, there may be many more such deviations from general laws, especially in that sealed book, some pages of which have been recently read—the bottom of the great deep. It may here be repeated that Dr. Carpenter has shown, from the results of the experience of the deep-sea sounding expedition, that there are many things in the great depths of the ocean which we dreamt not of in our philosophy, and that that philosophy in some respects has been hitherto very grossly in error. The portentous calculations of millions of years, based upon certain geological appearances, turn out

---

* Professor Ansted's "Ionian Islands," chap. xi.

to be fallacious, and life and vision at the bottom of the great deep, pronounced to be impossible, has now become an unquestionable fact.

We have, however, good reason for doubting declarations of the "impossible" by scientific men; for even in matters within the purview of science they have been grossly mistaken. Sir H. Davy condemned the proposal of lighting towns with gas; Dr. Lardner demonstrated that a steamer could not cross the Atlantic; and railway locomotive speed was ridiculed as impossible by many of the principal members of the engineering profession. Worst of all, perhaps, was the opposition raised by some of the most eminent "scientific men" of medical science to the use of ether as an anæsthetic, the greatest possible boon to suffering humanity. The circular issued to the medical officers in the Crimean campaign, recommending them not to make use of chloroform in operations, on the pretence (which seems like a grim joke) that pain is a wholesome stimulant, is sufficient to caution us against implicit faith in science. Sir Charles Lyell has, however, in his description of Etna,* pronounced that "No general deluge can have occurred in the forest zone of Etna since the lateral cones were thrown up; for few, if any, of these heaps of loose scoriæ could fail to have been swept away by a great flood, and all of them would have exhibited some signs of denudation." No doubt a great rush of water would probably have washed away all or part of them; but the description of the Flood in Genesis seems to imply a gradual submersion, for it

* "Principles," chap. xxvi. pp. 46, 47.

was to rain forty days and forty nights, after which the " rain from heaven was restrained;" or, according to Dr. Kalisch, "assuaged," "and the waters decreased continually from before the seventh month, and were dried up on the first of the first month of the following year," a period of from between five and six months. Therefore, according to the description in Genesis, there is reason to suppose a gradual subsidence of the water, and not any such violent rush of water, either in its rising or falling. Supposing the surface of the Mediterranean had risen above these cones, and that the Straits of Gibraltar were then formed to let out the waters; even in that case the water would have subsided so gradually at the distance of Etna from Gibraltar, as not to affect these cones, especially if covered, as they may have been, with vegetation (and who can say they were not so covered?) which, Sir C. Lyell says in the same place, protects them from waste by rain or wind. Again, can it be affirmed that they were not much larger originally than now, and have not been subject to waste? Again, if snow covered them, and not water, they may have lost little or nothing of their first dimensions. I cannot, therefore, see that these lateral cones of Etna, if then in existence, afford any argument against a general deluge. Dr. Kalisch* has made use of the cones of scoriæ in the volcanic region of Auvergne for a similar argument against a general deluge, but he seems not to have been aware that Sidonius Apollinaris and Avitus incidentally relate the great devastation created by an eruption of

* "Historical and Critical Commentary on the Old Testament," vol. i. p. 143.

some kind or other of the volcanoes of Auvergne in the sixth century. Extracts from those writers to that effect may be seen in the *Quarterly Review*, in article, "The ancient Laws and Institutes of England," No. 148, p. 281. It is therefore perfectly possible that these very cones of scoriæ may not have been thrown up until long after the Deluge, always remembering how very recent are the records and traditions of the country. From the ignorance of Dr. Kalisch, and not of him alone in this case, we observe that we must not place reliance upon the "memory of man."

Vitruvius informs us, long before the first historic eruption of Vesuvius, that "It is however said, that in former times fires under Vesuvius existed in abundance, and thence evolved flames about the fields.* As far as

* "Vitruvius," Gwilt's translation, p. 41.

man is concerned, Italy was, in the times of Vitruvius, an ancient country compared with countries north of the Alps; it is not therefore surprising that no record should have been preserved of the active state of volcanoes or volcanic regions in the north. If written tradition may so easily be forgotten, how much more is it the case with oral tradition? For aught we know, therefore, northern volcanoes, such as the Eifel, may have been active at no very early period of the earth's history.

Dr. Kalisch raises as another objection the immensity of time required for the excavation by the rivers of their channels through basaltic rocks 150 feet high. A reply to this objection is to be found in Sir C. Lyell's description of the Simeto, which it will be as well to repeat: "In the course therefore of about two centuries the Simeto has eroded a passage from fifty to several hundred feet wide, and in some parts forty to fifty feet deep;" he adds, that the lava cut through "consists of a compact homogeneous mass of hard blue rock." It does not appear, therefore, Dr. Kalisch is right in assuming such an immensity of time for the work of the river. Little faith, indeed, as I have endeavoured to show, can be placed in these calculations of immense periods of time.

Hugh Miller's suggestions with reference to the Deluge, the great subsidence of the earth in the region of the Caspian Sea—and his suggestion ought to be treated with the greatest respect—may be a solution of the problem of the Deluge. But if it be true, as affirmed by many geologists, that such

* Lyell's "Principles," &c. vol. i. p. 357.

changes in level of the earth's surface are so continually going on that we are to consider the earth, and not the sea, unstable; and besides these changes, when we consider the other dislocations, subsidences from earthquakes, and other causes to which the earth's surface is subjected, of which we have frequent examples in our own days, and which must obliterate the traces of the past, we cannot expect to find any direct evidence of the Deluge, more especially with our scanty knowledge of that part of the earth where we suppose it to have taken place. However, without giving any forced or unnatural interpretation of expressions in the archaic language of the Pentateuch, and only applying the same latitude of interpretation to them as we are compelled to do in other instances in the same book, we may have good reason to think that the objection raised by some scientific men, and by some geologists, are not borne out either by their criticisms or by the facts of geology, and the conjectures they found upon them. That the glacial period, which Professor Charles Martens* actually supposes, rightly or wrongly, to have taken place subsequently to mankind's appearance on earth, may have been the period of the Deluge, is at all events a probable method of accounting for the Noachian Deluge related in a book of unequalled authority, and for the all but universal tradition of mankind. We may therefore confidently believe that the obscure and difficult readings of the geological book of Nature are not inconsistent with the relation of the Deluge in the Bible—a book containing, as Professor Tyndal elo-

* "Revue des Deux Mondes," 1867.

quently says, "words of imperishable wisdom, and with examples of moral grandeur unmatched elsewhere in the history of the human race."

THE MOSAIC COSMOGONY.

AT the risk of being numbered with "bibliolaters, pietists, and old women of both sexes," among whom, however, I should find myself in first-rate scientific company, I must avow a sincere belief in the inspired character of the Old Testament, with its "words of imperishable wisdom and with examples of moral grandeur unmatched elsewhere in the history of the human race," the more, as it has been attested by the New Testament, for which I entertain, if possible, a still greater veneration and belief. Certain clergymen indeed seem to ignore the fact, forgetful of the words of the Saviour,

"If they hear not Moses and the prophets, neither will they be persuaded though one rose from the dead." Also, "For had ye believed Moses, ye would have believed me: for he wrote of me. But if ye believe not his writings, how shall ye believe my words?" That any clergyman of the Church of England, with a common sense of honour, honesty, and truth, can retain the advantages, position, and emoluments of that Church, the doctrines of which he has sworn to teach, while perverting or denying them — betraying the castle he bound himself to defend—is the disgrace of the present day, supported and encouraged as it is by so many laymen, who, if they like the treachery, should in common honesty detest the traitor, ready as they would be to punish as a swindler or traitor the ignorant man who takes money on false pretences, or the soldier who betrays his post. Some of these reverend gentlemen we have heard of insinuating that in these days no one is prepared to undergo martyrdom. They have spoken falsely for others, as Bishop Patteson has recently borne witness. They ignore the many who, in the strength of their convictions, are continually risking their health and lives in battling with deadly fevers, prepared for a martyrdom unheeded by the world, but they will not even sacrifice the good things of this world to their convictions—a base and contemptible conclusion, as every honest *thinker* (to use the present scientific cant expression) must surely acknowledge. The offence given to the feelings of veneration for the Bible is touchingly expressed in the Jewish answer to Colenso's mischievous and often childish objections, discussed and refuted ages ago by writers of their persuasion. Sharing in these feelings, I propose to add a few considerations to the many which have been so ably and so often adduced to show that there is no such inconsistency as has been pretended by some of our professors between the cosmogony of Moses and the discoveries of science.

It must be admitted that our knowledge of the language of the Bible, and of the habits, customs, and expressions of thought of the ancient people with which it deals, cannot possibly be so complete as to enable us to interpret satisfactorily certain idiomatic expressions and allusions, or even to understand the precise meaning of some words in the Bible. Many difficulties of the kind may be observed in every Hebraistic commentary of the Old Testament, and indeed occasionally in the New, as in all other ancient writings in dead languages; nevertheless the knowledge we have is quite sufficient to enable us to appreciate their value and to derive all essential advantage from them, whether they be sacred or profane. If, on the one hand, we have the authority of science—not however always a certain, unquestionable authority, for new are often setting aside former discoveries or theories—we have, on the other, the strongest evidence of the more than human origin of the Bible. We have, therefore, good reason for assuming that any apparent and absolute discrepancy, if any there be, between undoubted facts in Nature as discovered by science, and such facts as are stated in the Mosaic cosmogony, is due to a wrong interpretation of its meaning. Whatever amount of scientific knowledge Moses and the Egyptians may have possessed, it cannot be questioned that, as we have the advantage of all the knowledge of the past, our scientific acquirements must necessarily be very much greater; but that the Egyptians had a certain amount of scientific knowledge their remains of a very early date testify in various ways. It is also possible that the gross and monstrous idolatry of the Egyptians was the gradual growth of superstition, if Lucian on the Syrian goddess is to be believed, for he says, "The Assyrians imbibed their doctrines (the doctrines of the Egyptians), and built temples, in which they also placed statues and idols, of which the Egyptians had none in former ages." There is therefore reason to suppose that Moses, whether he wrote the first chapter of Genesis, or set his imprimatur on the writings of others, did not derive his science, astronomy especially, from "mere optical appearance," as Dr. Kalisch will have it. The Jehovist and Elohist theories are very ingenious, but doubtful, as the sacred names are in places found in close proximity, and, after all, these readings may be nothing more than what we might find in a modern author who might use indiscriminately the words "God," "the Lord," or the "Holy One" in the same work. The great paramount object of the Book of Genesis is, the Revelation of One Almighty God the Creator of all things, clothed in the simplest form perhaps of which the marvellous work of creation is capable, for the comprehension of all men, and not for that of the few scientific units among them. Libraries of books would be insufficient to explain it, and they would be unintelligible to the mass of mankind. When we consider the idolatry of the world in general, with its abominable and often cruel rites, and the multifarious and conflicting views of philosophers of all times, the necessity of such a revelation is apparent. No human being could, without inspiration from heaven, give a true account of the great work of creation. In so concise a description of this complicated and marvellous work, we can only expect to find in it the largest generalisations, any exceptions to which would of course remain unrecorded.

"In the beginning God created the heaven and the earth." Before geology existed as a science these words were considered to refer to a period antecedent to the state of the earth as described in the second verse—"And (or but) the earth was without form, and void; and darkness was upon the face of the deep: and the Spirit of God moved upon the face of the waters." * Dr. Kalisch, in his "Historical and Critical Commentary of the Old Testament," pronounces that "The connecting particle *and* [at the beginning of the verse] expresses here necessarily immediate sequence. . . . It is, in a word, utterly impossible to separate the two first verses and to suppose between them an immense interval of time." Now as we find that same particle, *and*, in our translation at the beginning of nearly every verse or sentence in Genesis, that in various instances it is merely a "connecting particle," to signify a continuation of the narrative, without any such "immediate sequence," and that this particular particle,

* There is some reason to think St. Peter held this view, for he says that "by the Word of God the heavens were of old, and the earth standing out of the water and in the water."

and, only happens to be the first in the whole Bible, it seems anything but "utterly impossible to separate the two first verses and to suppose between them an immense interval of time." In the Vulgate (the translation of St. Jerome, who was assisted by rabbis of his day), the rendering of this word, *and*, is "autem," *but;* and in the Septuagint translation we find the word καὶ, *and*, used as in our version everywhere except in the beginning of this second verse; there we find Ἡ δὲ γῆ ἦν ἀόρατος, &c., "but," or, "for the earth was invisible,—&c.," it would almost appear for the purpose of marking that there was no such "immediate sequence" as Dr. Kalisch dogmatically assumes. It is, therefore, a fair interpretation of the text to consider that the first verse has reference to the beginning of creation, the second to a certain period when the created earth was in a chaotic state preparatory to its adaptation for the requirements of man and of animate nature contemporaneous with him, in the same manner as geology shows the existence of other periods adapted to other organic creatures. For it appears that certain changes or revolutions have at different times altered the condition of the earth's surface; that in the earliest periods there probably prevailed a large amount of intense heat, mineral matter in a state of fusion furnishing the various materials of which the earth's crust was afterwards to be composed; that at one period animal life was confined to mollusks alone—creations, be it observed, totally distinct from those of subsequent periods; at another period fishes, birds, and reptiles were introduced; in the last period mammals; and, finally, man. Not only are these various periods distinguishable from the evidence of their fossil witnesses, but also from other general considerations. A much greater heat on the earth's surface must have prevailed when immense masses of plutonic or igneous rocks, granite, &c., penetrated the sedimentary rocks and strata of the primary and secondary period, scarcely at all touching the tertiary, and not reaching at all the more recent periods. The truth of this inference of a greater amount of heat is confirmed by the evidence of a vast amount of tropical vegetation (distinct, however, from our tropical vegetation) discovered in many regions of the world, arctic, temperate, and tropical.* The fossils of each period are

* Humboldt, whose knowledge and experience of volcanoes and their action was so great, says in the "Cosmos," vol. i. p. 259, "The active volcanoes of the present time communicat-

so distinctly marked that the geologist can at once, speaking generally, declare the period to which each fossil belongs.

We have therefore good geological reason for supposing that the earth, described as "without form, and void," may then have been passing through that revolution which produced an earth's surface adapted to the existence of the present series of animate life, including man, the Creator's most exalted creature—the last geological period. From geology again, we learn that though essentially different forms of organic life were in existence at the several periods, in some cases

---

ing with the air by craters, must not be confounded with those older eruptions of granite, quartzose, porphyry, and euphotide, through open but speedily closed fissures (forming veins) which occur in the older transition strata. *Vide* also pp. 274-5, showing the distinction.

the resemblance of the newer to the older forms is preserved; and whether any of them survived the different revolutions of the earth, which may have been the case with respect to some of them, especially marine creations, as we now know that they can exist at profound depths and in darkness; or whether after each such revolution a new took the place of the old creation, preserving in some cases the same form, in others a similarity of type or form, we may conjecture, but never be able to discover, still less dogmatically to assert. As an illustration of my meaning as to such new creations, I compare them with the works of a Palissy, or a Wedgwood, or a Minton, who gave up old forms, retaining the general order of construction, and adopted new forms in their creations. I have already adverted to the absurd objection of the supposition of caprice in creation. We may be thankful for the great enjoyment vouchsafed to us by the infinite variety of vegetation, indeed of all Nature—a variety which might equally be attributed to such caprice. We may, in fact, see many a purpose in the convulsions which have acted upon the surface of the earth in these different periods, and which, in the words of Von Humboldt, have covered "the dry land of either half of the globe with a beautiful abundance of individual forms," and been "conducive to free at least the greater portion of it from the blank of uniformity which appears to cramp and impoverish both the physical and intellectual powers of man."* We have also evidence of times of a more uniform temperature, perhaps an intense heat on the surface

* "Cosmos," vol. i. p. 323.

of the globe, and, comparatively near the time when man first appeared, a period of intense cold. "Hence, independently of the indications of a more equally diffused and warmer temperature in older times than at the present day, such large erratic blocks are in themselves direct testimonials of that intense cold which it is believed was principally due to the increase of great elevated masses of land especially characteristic of the quasi-modern period." *

The "darkness over the face of the deep" may have been the lost light of the sun, or, on a large scale, a darkness similar to that which, on a small scale, hangs over the Peruvian plains, thus described by Humboldt in his "Cosmos" †—"A thick mist covers the sky for

---

* Murchison's "Siluria," p. 505.   † Vol. iii. pp. 86, 87.

several months during the season called 'el tiempo della Garua.' No planet, not even one of the brightest stars of the southern hemisphere, neither Canopus, nor the Southern Cross, nor the two bright stars of the Centaur, are visible. Often one can hardly conjecture the place of the moon. If occasionally during the daytime it is possible to distinguish the outlines of the sun's disk, it appears rayless, shorn of its beams, as if viewed through a coloured glass, &c. . . . . A grave consideration is suggested by the character of this atmospheric stratum, which is *so unfavourable to the transmission of light*, and so unfitted for electric discharges, that thunder and lightning are unknown there, and which veils the plains in constant mist, while above, the Cordilleras raise aloft, free and unclouded, their elevated plains and snowy summits. According to the conjectures which modern geology leads us to form respecting the ancient history of our atmosphere, its primitive state, in respect to composition and density, must have been little favourable to the passage of light. If then we think of the many processes which may have been in operation in the early state of the crust of the globe, in the separation of solid, liquid, and gaseous substances, we are impressed with a view of how possible it must have been that we should have been subjected to conditions and circumstances very different from those which we actually enjoy. We might have been surrounded by an untransparent atmosphere, which, while but little unfavourable to the growth of several kinds of vegetation, would have veiled from us the whole starry firmament."

Here, then, we have a philosophical conjecture, harmonizing not only with the Mosaic description of the state of the earth's surface before the fourth day, but also with that of the third day, when vegetation was to appear before the appearance of the light of the sun. It must not be supposed that Von Humboldt had any intention of suggesting such a harmony between his conjectures and the statements in the first chapter of Genesis, for in the first volume, p. 288, he speaks of "geology, now finally abstracted, on the Continent at least, from Semitic influences." We have no reason to envy France at all events, where the absence of "Semitic influences" has largely contributed to that utter absence of principle which has produced so many grievous wars and revolutions, with their bitter fruits and abundant stock of misery for its inhabitants. But, further on, it will be seen that many other suggestions—on scientific principles—may be adduced to account for the darkness over the face of the deep.

"And God said, Let there be light: and there was light" (otherwise translated "Let light be, and light was"). "And God saw the light, that it was good: and God divided the light from the darkness. And God called the light Day, and the darkness he called Night. And the evening and the morning were the first day," or, "Evening was, and morning was."

It is remarkable that Moses, living with a people and among nations who made the sun an object of worship, attributing to it all light and life, should not have taken the common human view, and described light as an emanation from the sun. On the contrary, we learn the truth from Moses, that there is light wholly independent of the sun. Nevertheless, the sun may have been at this time in existence without light, but retaining its power of attraction to keep the earth in its orbit, yet having lost the light which shone on former periods of the earth's history. Many stars or suns have shone for years, the light of which has entirely disappeared. Who can pretend to assert that such an event may not at that time of a new creation have taken place with respect to our sun? Dark spots have covered vast surfaces of the sun, dark spots very many diameters larger than that of the earth. It is possible that these dark spots (supposed openings in the photosphere) may so have covered, either partially or completely, its surface, as to render its light imperceptible on the earth. The undulatory theory (undulations of light crossing and meeting one another in infinite directions) has replaced the Newtonian theory of light, and a supposed universal æther has been conjectured—supported by the observed contraction of the periods of Encke's comet. But as to what light really is we know not; we have only discovered the mode of its transmission, so far at least as to give a satisfactory interpretation of its action. Schellen, in his "Spectrum Analysis," p. 9, says, "The immediate cause of the luminosity of a flame has not yet been fully ascertained, notwithstanding the many investigations that have been made with this object." We have therefore reason to admire the Mosaic account of the first renewed appearance of light, in its scientific aspect, always supposing that account to apply to the creation of the earth's surface for the last geological human period. We have no reason to take the words "let there be light" as signifying a first creation of light (it is not said, God *created* light as He "created the heaven and the earth"), but in the sense of "let there be light upon the earth," which does not preclude the idea of a pre-existence of light, to which, at the time we have now under consideration, the earth may have been insensible. Schellen again says (*ibid.*, p. 55), "Light is not therefore a separate substance, but only the vibration of a substance which, according to its various forms of motion, generates light, heat, or electricity."

Every one in the time of Moses, as now, must have been aware that day and night are owing to the presence and absence of the sun's light. Accordingly we find in the fourteenth verse, "Let there be lights in the firmament of the heaven to divide the day from the night," &c. The words, therefore, "And God called the light day, and the darkness he called night," must either be taken parenthetically, or the light of the sun must have been at that time not either in quality or intensity identical with that referred to in the sixteenth verse. Of the possibility of such a state of things we have evidence in the fact that not only have stars or suns been seen to increase their lights gradually to that of stars of the first magnitude, and then to die away again into darkness, but these suns also have visibly changed their colours, or, in other words, their light, and any satellite planets they may have must have suffered accordingly.* So the first light of the sun, as mentioned in this verse,

---

* Humboldt says: "Dark cosmical bodies may suddenly shine forth afresh by a resumed luminous process."—(Vol. iii. p. 152.)

may have proceeded from a photosphere different to that it attained subsequently, and might be, perhaps, more adapted to the growth of the *first* germs of the vegetation the earth was to produce on the third day of creation, which will presently be considered.*

"And the evening and the morning were the first day." The days of creation seem merely to point out that at certain six different times the various works of creation, or the fiats of the Almighty, were sent forth; nor have we any right to assume that by the six days is meant six consecutive days of one week, a view derived perhaps from the

* Mr. Denison remarks on the words "let there be light," that "no other words would have been equally correct; for it is now ascertained that light is not a thing to be created like water, but rather a state of things like fire or noise."—("Astronomy without Mathematics," p. 28.)

statement in the fourth commandment—" For in six days the Lord made heaven and earth," &c.; but surely these six days of the commandment may be considered only as representing symbolically the six times at which the fiats of creation went forth, as the seventh day was to perpetuate the remembrance of the rest from creation, a rest continued to the best of our knowledge up to the present day. We are nowhere told that creation took place in one week.

But although we can take in a general idea of a creation of the earth, much as we often see the material results of a mental process without the smallest conception of the manner in which they were brought about, the *modus operandi*, or what were the processes of creation, are, and ever must be, *tabula rasa* to us. Whether creation signifies the creation of the first germ or protoplasm of any creature or its full development, we are not told, and perhaps, certainly as far as the mass of mankind are concerned, could not understand if told. All therefore we have to understand by the Mosaic description of creation is the simple fact of creation at certain times or periods, but the how, and the how long or how short the completion of each separate work, we are not told, and the solution of the mystery can only be a matter of conjecture. Even in the creations or inventions of man, such, for instance, as the extraordinary calculating machine of Mr. Babbage, it might be said that it was created when elaborated in his mind or sketched on paper, supposing that he were certain that it would work when constructed, as in the case of the creations of an Almighty power. I think, however, that when we come to the consideration of the text describing, or rather announcing, the appearance of vegetation, we shall be led to the conclusion that that text actually conveys the idea that the work of the third day was the work of time, and not of a period of twenty-four hours.

"And God said, Let there be a firmament in the midst of the waters, and let it divide the waters from the waters. And God made the firmament, and divided the waters which were under the firmament from the waters which were above the firmament: and it was so. And God called the firmament Heaven. And the evening and the morning were the second day." The word *firmament* is translated *expanse* by Kalisch and others: it is therefore evident that we are not acquainted with the exact meaning of the word, whatever meaning the Septuagint (στερέωμα) or the Vulgate may have given to it. We may, however, infer that it means the creation of the atmosphere, which is saturated with the vapour of water, and shows that, in the words of "Cosmos,"* "Our planet has two coverings or envelopes—one general, the atmosphere, as elastic fluid; and one particular, only locally distributed, bounding the solid, and thereby giving it its figure, the sea." The atmosphere was thus prepared for the organic life which was to come, different in some respects perhaps from the atmosphere of the past, for it is supposed by some philosophers, Humboldt among others,† that the atmosphere contained a greater amount of carbonic acid, to account for the great luxuriance of vegetation in the former world, as

* Vol. i. p. 308. † Vol. i. p. 270.

evidenced by the coal formation found in every latitude of the earth. That the Bible was not intended to teach astronomy any more than chemistry or the various ologies, but to teach as its sole object the duty of man to his Creator, is evident. We do not find fault with the astronomer because he does not treat of other sciences as well as his own. The term *firmament* and *heaven* we may therefore presume to be an expression used figuratively, like that of the "vault of heaven," employed repeatedly by Humboldt, yet we do not suppose he considered the heavens a vault; or as we read in the Bible of the earth "opening her mouth"—a figurative expression. If under the term *waters* we may include vapour, which I conceive we have every right philologically to do, the description of Moses is very much what we know of the atmosphere, and it seems more probable that a man, living under the glorious transparency of an Egyptian or an Eastern atmosphere, would not have imagined the existence of any intermediate stratum between earth and heaven.

"And God said, Let the waters under the heaven be gathered together unto one place, and let the dry land appear: and it was so. And God called the dry land Earth; and the gathering together of the waters called he Seas: and God saw that it was good."

In this very general description of a stupendous event, we may suppose particular exceptions; and, as I have before said, we have no right to assume that these words imply an instantaneous operation concluded in one day. There may have been islands scattered here and there: the peaks of the

Himalayas, Andes, or Alps may have then stood above the waters; but we gather from geology the unquestionable fact that, at some time or times, great portions of the earth were either uplifted from the waters, or the waters were lowered. The cretaceous formations and other masses of strata containing the fossils of marine creatures incontestably show that they were once beneath the waters, though now uplifted high above them. What we know, therefore, of the earth's surface is amply sufficient to show that the Mosaic account is, in this respect, in accordance with geological science.

"And God said, Let the earth bring forth grass, the herb yielding seed, and the fruit-tree yielding fruit after his kind, whose seed is in itself, upon the earth: and it was so. And the earth brought forth grass, and herb yielding seed after his kind, and the tree yielding fruit, whose seed was in itself, after his kind: and God saw that it was good. And the evening and the morning were the third day."

It is again remarkable that Moses, seeing, as we all see, how necessary are the light and heat of the sun for the growth of vegetation, should, if guided only by natural human intelligence, have placed the creation, or the first production, of a new vegetation, before the light of the sun was made to shine upon the earth. It is not said here that God *created* grass, &c., but "let the earth bring forth," which may imply that the seeds of vegetation were already in the earth, waiting for the atmospheric conditions suitable to their growth. We cannot know what were these conditions before or after that time, but we know that the vegetation of former periods of the earth's history was very different, and that the atmospheric conditions provided for them must have been very different from those of our period. The almost universal coal-measures, for instance, afford an unmistakable proof that the same climate prevailed in arctic, temperate, and tropical latitudes in both hemispheres, although it was impossible that these latitudes could have enjoyed the same amount of the sun's light or heat. We have therefore satisfactory proof of vegetation of the richest character flourishing under a minimum of that light and heat; or again, to use the words of Humboldt, "We might have been surrounded by an untransparent atmosphere which, while but little unfavourable to the growth of vegetation, would have veiled from us the whole starry firmament." In this part of the history of creation we may also observe how general is the description, for Moses only mentions grass, herbs, and fruit-trees; yet it is impossible to suppose he was not aware of the many other trees, water-plants, seaweeds, &c., which he does not mention. So in other descriptions we can only find generalisations of the largest kind.

As we cannot know in what manner or by what process the earth, bare of all vegetation, was converted into the state of a beautiful garden, such as we now see it, we may only conjecture that the full light of the sun was not suited to its first coming into existence. The sun's heat creates the storm and fills the atmosphere, by evaporation, with clouds and rain. We may conjecture that incipient vegetation, especially on hill and mountain-sides, could not have borne the denuding effects of the storm and the rain, as we now know that (as I have before shown) hill-sides and large tracts, once deprived of their forests, are laid bare by them of all vegetation, with the destruction of vegetation at the base of the hills and mountains. Accordingly, we find in the fifth and sixth verse of the second chapter—" For the Lord God had not caused it to rain upon the earth, and there was not a man to till the ground. But there went up a mist from the earth, and watered the whole face of the ground "—a gentle irrigation, more suited to the incipient life of plants. Here again these words seem to imply a slow, continuous action. The fiat went forth on the third day, but the sense of the relation seems to imply that the work of the mist was not completed in the course of one day of twenty-four hours, although no one can pretend to say that the germination of the vegetation of the whole earth did not, or could not, take place in the course of one day at its first appearance. That the vegetable kingdom should have preceded the appearance on earth of the animal kingdom seems consonant with reason, inasmuch as the vast proportion of the animal world derive their subsistence and life from the vegetable world, which, according to Humboldt, " far exceeds the animal world on the face of the globe."* He indeed says:—"Nothing seems to testify, as . . . . it has been assumed, that vegetable life was awakened sooner than animal life upon the face of the old earth, and this was brought about or determined by that."† And his reason for this notion is an extraordinary

* "Cosmos," vol. i p. 377. † Vol. i. p. 297.

one:—"The existences of races of men in the very northern polar zones, who subsist on the flesh of fish and seals and whales, is enough of itself to assure us of the possibility of living without vegetable matter of any kind;"* that is to say, that because the omnivorous animal, man, is endowed with a constitution enabling him to exist under all conditions of food and climate, as well without vegetable as without animal food, therefore we are to assume, without any proof or experience, that creatures purely herbivorous can exist without vegetable matter. And this, because we have not discovered in the Silurian or Devonian strata much fossil vegetation. Mr. Philips, however, in the "Geology of Oxford," p. 74, enumerates four kinds of plants in the Silurian period. Many circum-

* Humboldt, p. 298.

stances may account for the absence—which, after all, is but apparent—of more kinds of plants and greater quantities in the ancient strata. But as we are now dealing with the human geological period, we can have no doubt of the infinite number of the creatures of our earth who live upon its flora, and who supply food for the carnivora. The true scientific view would therefore seem to correspond with that of Genesis, which places the creation of the flora before that of the fauna of the earth.

"And God said, Let there be lights in the firmament of the heaven to divide the day from the night; and let them be for signs, and for seasons, and for days, and years: and let them be for lights in the firmament of the heaven to give light upon the earth: and it was so. And God made two great lights; the greater light to rule the day, and the lesser light to rule the night: He made the stars also. And God set them in the firmament of the heaven to give light upon the earth, and to rule over the day and over the night, and to divide the light from the darkness: and God saw that it was good. And the evening and the morning were the fourth day."

The production of the lights, and that God made the two great lights, are separate clauses, as it were; the first showing that the sun's light was made to shine in its full force upon the earth, the second to be taken parenthetically, as if it were said, "God caused the sun's light to shine on earth by day, the moon's by night—for God had made the sun and moon, the stars also." The words *He made*, in the sentence, "*He made* the stars also," are not in the original. That the ancient readers of this passage held that it signified a former creation, as far as the stars are concerned, we have every reason to think with more modern authorities; for though the passage in Job, "the morning stars sang together" when God "laid the foundations of the earth," is a poetical one, it could hardly have been said if the writer supposed the creation of the earth to have preceded that of the stars. Perhaps, also, it was especially declared that not only did God command "Let there be light," &c., but also emphatically that God *made* or created the "two great lights," &c., to guard against the idolatrous worship of the sun and moon, the sun being probably, even in the time of Moses, by the Egyptian and almost all heathen nations of old, and even to this day, an object of worship with some of the peoples of the earth. In the concise description of this wondrous work of creation, we only find its primary objects, as far as the earth is concerned; Moses, or the person whose words he has adopted—if indeed this part of the Pentateuch is a compilation—must have been aware of the fact that the sun has other important functions. Could he, living in Egypt, have possibly been unaware that heat as well as light proceeded from the sun, that that heat without moisture produced a desert, and with it the richest vegetation? It is absurd therefore to find fault with the description, from the absence of any references to certain other properties of the sun and moon, which, whether they were known or not to Moses, would have been out of place in this grand, general, and concise description, and would have required a volume to enumerate so as to be intelligible. The creation of immense masses of matter such as the sun (in size many times the diameter of the earth) has undoubtedly had for its object a beneficial influence upon the earth, and for the myriads of living souls and animated beings dwelling upon it. The sun may or may not have the same influence in other planets, for we know nothing more than that it preserves those planets in their orbits. Of the moon's influence we know little more than that in addition to its light, its attraction, together with that of the sun, affects the tides of the ocean; and we have some reason to conjecture that that great mass of matter is a fearful waste of volcanoes, without atmosphere or (perhaps) water, and therefore without life, such at least as exists on this earth.

So far therefore as we know, the moon *was* created for the principal purpose of shedding light upon the earth at night. Professor Tyndal treats "this little sand-grain of earth" as nothing compared with the infinite universe of worlds of matter: and so it is; but we must not forget that this "little sand-grain" contains myriads of living, intelligent, immortal souls, which in their Creator's view may surely be of more importance than masses of inert matter such as the sun and moon. Two sharks, it is said, were conversing together after making a meal upon the dead body of a seaman fallen from the *Great Eastern*. "What a wonder," said shark A, "that that monstrous edifice, many times bigger than those troublesome whales, should be for the use of such miserable creatures as the one we have just dined upon!"—

"Pooh, nonsense!" answered shark B; "it is absurd to suppose so great, so wonderful a construction to be for the use of such wretched little animals."

Thus far then we have good reason to believe that in the grand simplicity of the Mosaic description of the work of creation there is nothing contradictory to the determinations of science, but rather a coincidence with them.

"And God said, Let the waters bring forth abundantly the moving creature that hath life, and fowl that may fly above the earth in the open firmament of heaven. And God created great whales, and every living creature that moveth, which the waters brought forth abundantly, after their kind, and every winged fowl after his kind, and God saw that it was good. And God blessed them, saying, Be fruitful, and multiply, and fill the waters in the seas, and let fowl multiply in the earth. And the evening and the morning were the fifth day."

From the researches of geologists we gather that great changes have taken place on the earth's surface which are divided into periods. The vegetable world of one period is very different from that of another period. The same may be said of the animal world. Races and species have wholly disappeared and given place to wholly different species. Both the flora and fauna of the earth in some of these periods show from their presence in all parts of the earth that its climate must have been different from the climate of our, the latest, period. If, therefore, such changes have taken place on the face of the earth, we may with reason believe it to be more than probable that such a change took place when the present organic life on earth, including mankind, was created. We can never know what were the first processes of creation. Some ancient cosmogonies pretend to give an account of such processes, and some modern scientific men have been or are engaged in inventing theories to explain them; but all are wanting in the essential element of historical or geological evidence in explanation of the fact that no such processes have ever been known to mankind, or why they should have so long ceased to operate. But whatever may have been those first processes, all that the words of Genesis demand of us is the belief that all animal life was created by the Almighty. We might also assume that the exceptional mention of the creation of the whale, to an inhabitant of

Egypt not a familiar mammal, may be to show that this creation of the fifth day was the creation of the last great periodic change of the earth's surface, the whale being unknown hitherto in the fossil world of the earlier periods. And because we trace a few forms passing into the last period from the preceding one, we have no right to consider this fact evidence against a new creation; for either it is possible that the former forms of life should have perished and have been removed, or that some of them may have survived exceptionally the general destruction—the very general and concise nature of this history of creation naturally excluding exceptions, exceptions which, geologically, for the most part are to be found among the lower forms of life. Our absolute ignorance of the *modus operandi* of a first creation of anything whatever—whether male and female were created at the same time; whether a germ, protoplasm, or primordial form was the first seed of life; or whether the process was a long or a short one, we can never know. If a long one, there is nothing in the account given in Genesis to prevent such an interpretation. All that we are told is, that creative energy was exercised in the creation of animal life on the fifth day of its exercise. It is possible that the process was long, but equally possible that it was instantaneous for aught we know. As I have said before, we have no right to interpret the six days as days of one week. Even in the English language, events may surely be said to have taken place in six days without necessarily implying the six days of one week. It would be no error in language to say that Professor So-and-so lectured on light one day, on the atmosphere a second day, on vegetation a third day, &c., although such lectures were delivered only once a month, or with any other intervals of time between them. Whether genera or species which abhor intermixture ever intermixed, or whether each genus, species, or race were distinct creations, the first chapter of Genesis does not inform us. All we learn from it is the fact that the Almighty God was their Creator, a fact unquestioned by the greatest of our scientific men.

"And God said, Let us make man in our image, after our likeness: and let them have dominion over the fish of the sea, and over the fowl of the air, and over the cattle, and over all the earth, and over every creeping thing that creepeth upon the earth. So God created man in his own image, in the image of God created he him; male and female created he them."

Here again we have the simple declaration of man's creation by the Almighty without the smallest reference to the process of his creation, leaving that entirely to speculation, which may be characterised as idle. I have endeavoured to show that the arguments for the great antiquity of man are very fallacious. Geology, however, as far as its revelations extend, shows unmistakably that man was among the latest, as we learn in Genesis that he was the last of the creations of the Almighty. This geological fact is of such general application, that if we were to find in tertiary or even in secondary strata remains of man, or of his works, we should be justified in concluding their position was due to their fall into a fissure, the result of an earthquake or some other unknown cause, rather than that they should have been the relics of men who were living at the period of the stratum in which they might be found. This caution is requisite because it is not impossible that such remains may be discovered some day or other at any depth in the earth, although I am not aware of any such discovery of human relics as yet, notwithstanding the very great number of men and their works now in the bowels of the earth, buried in fissures caused by the earthquakes which appear to have shaken one part or other of the globe throughout all time.* This account of man's creation is in exact conformity with what we know of

* "Could we have daily news of the state of the whole of the earth's surface, we should, in all probability, become convinced that some point or another of this surface is ceaselessly shaken; that there is uninterrupted reaction of the interior upon the exterior going on."—("Cosmos," vol. i. p. 221.)

the results of geological research; and any conclusions, or rather conjectures, of science as to the manner or the process of creation, cannot in any way affect the simple statement of Genesis that man was the work of the Creator, whatever secondary laws they may think to discover in the process of his creation.

The mythophilosophical conjectures of the present day, pretending to an explanation of the first processes of the creation of organic beings, seem to be little more credible than the mythological descriptions of times past. To call them scientific seems altogether a misnomer, for true science is based upon indubitable fact, which cannot be gainsaid. The processes of creation we can never penetrate, and the attempts to do so smack very much of the scientific pedantry which assumes to explain all the inexplicable things in nature, not so utterly beyond the reach of our intelligence as the mystery of mysteries—Creation.

In the second chapter we find, "And the Lord God formed man of the dust of the ground." Any one wishing for the confirmation of science on this point, will find in the Kensington Museum the earthy substances of which, in their due proportions, his mortal body is composed. That Dr. Kalisch and other commentators should have considered this second chapter a second cosmogony, differing from the first, seems an unwarrantable misconstruction of the text. Can it be supposed that the writer or compiler of these two chapters should have deliberately contradicted himself, almost, one might say, in the same breath? The second chapter appears to be merely a recapitulation and amplification, with a few details of the first, or, according to the theory in "Adam and the Adamite," an account of the creation of Adam as distinguished from the men mentioned in the first chapter. Dr. Kalisch alleges that in the first chapter "the birds and beasts are created before man;" in the latter, or second chapter, "man before beasts and birds," because it is said in the nineteenth verse, "And out of the ground the Lord God formed every beast of the field," &c., having before said in the seventh verse, "And the Lord God formed man of the dust of the ground." The answer to this is to be found in the Vulgate translation of the nineteenth verse, "Formatis igitur Dominus Deus de humo cunctis animantibus terra," &c. ("The Lord God, therefore, having formed every living thing of the earth," &c.) It is therefore only a question of the tense which is to be given to the verb *formed*. As we find in the preface to the edition of the Vulgate of Clement VIII., "in hac tamen pervulgata sectione, sicut nonnulla consulto *mutata*, ita etiam alia, quæ mutanda videbantur, consulto immutata relicta sunt," the authenticity of the version is questionable, and the reading may not be trustworthy unless found in earlier copies. However, the Septuagint gives the same past signification to the word *formed*, ἔπλασε—καὶ ἔπλασεν ὁ Θεος ἔτι ἐκ τῆς γῆς πάντα τὰ θηρία, &c. Here there can be no doubt of the past signification of ἔπλασε, inasmuch as it is used in the fifteenth verse, καὶ ἔλαβε κύριος ὁ Θεος τὸν ἄνθρωπον ὃν ἔπλασε, which can only be translated "*had* made." The same word and tense, the first aoristic, ἔπλασεν, is used in the seventh verse. The versions, therefore, of these passages of the second chapter in the Vulgate and Septuagint seem certainly more rational than our authorised version.

The other arguments adduced for assuming the second chapter to contain another and a different cosmogony are satisfactorily nullified in Wordsworth's "Holy Bible."

Without presuming to give any dogmatic interpretation of the Mosaic account of Creation or of the Deluge, or to suppose that my view of the manner in which they are to be construed is the correct one, I hope to have shown, without any strained readings of the text, that the brief and majestic history of these two great events, in their relation to science, may coincide rather than conflict with scientific knowledge, wherever it can be brought to bear upon so concise, indefinite, and popular, as it may be called, relation of such a complicated work.

Well did St. Peter predict that scoffers should come, saying, "Where is the promise of his coming? for since the fathers fell asleep all things continue as they were from the beginning of creation." The Christian doctrine that it pleased God to set apart one nation of the earth through which His Will is communicated to mankind, is surely a doctrine with which *primá-facia* science cannot deal, and scientific men have neither right nor reason to reject. But this doctrine is supported by statements of miracles—*i.e.* of exceptions to general laws, including prophetic announcements. How could a proof be given to mankind of their divine commission to teach, except by the demonstration of powers beyond those of man? But miracles have been constantly mere impostures. Are not all human things subjected to imposture, and are we to reject all because of these impostures? Imposture is in fact nothing, as a rule, but the imitation or adulteration of truth. Science shows many instances of exceptions to general laws in the physical world. Why are we to suppose that some of these exceptions to physical laws, in the forms of miracles, may not have been ordained to enable the great and true religious teachers of mankind to prove that their mission was of God? Many of our greatest—the greatest, indeed—of our scientific men have been of this opinion; and, considering the untold and unnumbered material advantages science has conferred upon mankind, it is painful to see some of its professors arrayed in hostile attitude to religion; for without religion morality, truth, and virtue would be rarer than they are; and without morality, science and knowledge would be as likely to produce as much evil as good, to the misery of the human race, already sufficiently corrupted by their uncontrolled passions and the evil teaching of some so-called savans and scientific men—as St. Paul says, the "oppositions of science falsely so called." Babbage brought the doctrine of chances or probabilities to bear upon Hume's argument from probabilities against miracles, thus showing by a strict mathematical demonstration the fallacy of Hume's reasoning. He also shows a remarkable exception to, one would suppose, an unalterable mathematical law, a break in the continuity of a quasi-infinite series, such as miracles may be in the continuity of physical laws, of which we have anything but a perfect knowledge. With Babbage, Sir C. Bell, Sir H. Davy, Faraday, Newton, and Bacon, we may be comforted in the assurance that true science is not the antagonist of the Christian religion.

THE END.

Works by the Duke of Argyll.

The Reign of Law.
Crown 8vo, 6s.   People's Edition, limp cloth, 2s. 6d.

"There are few books in which a thoughtful reader will find more that he will desire to remember."—*Times.*
"Shows a breadth of thought, a freedom from prejudice, and a power of clear exposition rare in all ages and all countries. It is as unanswerable as it is attractive."—*Pall Mall Gazette.*
"A masterly book. . . . Strong, sound, mature, able thought from its first page to its last."—*Spectator.*
"The question with which this book deals is just the one which pious and practical minds find the most perplexing. . . . In the Duke of Argyll we miss none of the required faculties."—*Saturday Review.*
"The Duke of Argyll has made a real contribution towards the solution of a great problem, and has produced a book which would do credit to the calmest and most disengaged philosopher."—*Guardian.*

Primeval Man. An Examination
of Some Recent Speculations.   Crown 8vo, 4s. 6d.

"This volume is perhaps the most clear, graceful, pointed, and precise piece of ethical reasoning published for a quarter of a century. . . . Its great end is to show that it is impossible to pursue any investigation of man's history from the purely physical side. Its reasoning seems to us absolutely conclusive against the upholders of the 'natural selection' theory. . . . The book is worthy of a place in every library, as skilfully popularising science, and yet sacrificing nothing either of its dignity or of its usefulness."—*Nonconformist.*
"This book shows great knowledge, unusual command of language, and a true sense of the value of arguments. . . . It may be questioned, and even confuted, in some points, without losing any of its claims as a candid, clear, and high-minded discussion."—*Pall Mall Gazette.*

Iona.
With Illustrations.   Crown 8vo, 3s. 6d.

"Pleasantly and unaffectedly written, it is well fitted to discharge what we take to be the main object of such a work, that of guiding people to a subject and setting them to think about it. We are not ashamed to confess that we put down the Duke's little book with a wish to know more about Iona and St. Columba than we knew when we began it. We thank the Duke of Argyll for a pretty little book."—*Saturday Review.*

STRAHAN & CO., 56, LUDGATE HILL, LONDON.

www.ingramcontent.com/pod-product-compliance
Lightning Source LLC
Chambersburg PA
CBHW020326240426
43673CB00039B/927